# GOOD IN BED

*A Life in Queer Sex, Politics,
and Religion*

## by Brian Bouldrey

**ReQueered Tales**
Los Angeles • Toronto
2023

# Good in Bed

## *A Life in Queer Sex, Politics, and Religion*

### by Brian Bouldrey

First American edition: 2023

This edition: ReQueered Tales, November 2023

ReQueered Tales version 1.20
Kindle edition ASIN: B0CKLXZ2F4
Epub edition ISBN-13: 978-1-959902-04-1
Paperback edition ISBN-13: 978-1-959902-05-8
Hardcover edition ISBN-13: 978-1-951092-16-4

*For more information about current and future releases,
please contact us:*
E-mail: *requeeredtales@gmail.com*
Facebook (Like us!): www.facebook.com/ReQueeredTales
Twitter: @ReQueered
Instagram: www.instagram.com/requeered
Web: www.ReQueeredTales.com
Blog: www.ReQueeredTales.com/blog
Mailing list (Subscribe for latest news): https://bit.ly/RQTJoin

# Advance Praise for
# GOOD IN BED

"Bouldrey's *Good in Bed* is a delight. This is the sort of book that you never want to finish – you get to the last fifty pages and you want it to go on and on. There are so many trips to take with Brian, on the page and in the world, and you will be accompanied by that delightful, curious, and hilarious mind. You won't want to let go, and you'll trust him all along the way. Bouldrey writes, "To have such confidence, to be so sure of one's own ability and subject to spend a life devoted to one ever-growing project – even if it might not be a success – this is success in life."

— Julia Sweeney, *God Said Ha!*

"Warning: despite the title, do not read this book in bed. Because Brian Bouldrey can break your heart. Here, as Dostoevsky rubs shoulders with hard-core porn, laughter leads to tears (and vice versa). Shot through with a hard-won, wry humanity, Bouldrey writes like a funny, fallen angel – a wonderful companion for all who steer clear of the straight and narrow."

— Lesley Hazleton, *Agnostic: A Spirited Manifesto*

"Flip, hilarious, dead-on observant, mordant, and finally amazingly honest and sad. *Good in Bed* is an unexpected gift from a talented novelist. It's as delicious as tasting assorted chocolate bon-bons from a heart shaped velvet carton, while reading movie magazines and listening to the Go-Go's."

— Felice Picano, *Like People in History*

"Like the best post-coital pillow talk, Brian Bouldrey's *Good in Bed* is at once intimate, digressive, insightful, confessional, and witty. He's also quite erudite, capable of incorporating Kierkegaard and The Simpsons in a single paragraph, so be prepared for some cognitive pyrotechnics!"

— Alvin Orloff, *Vulgarian Rhapsody*

# Also by Brian Bouldrey

## FICTION

The Genius of Desire (1993)

Love, the Magician (2000)

The Boom Economy: Or, Scenes from Clerical Life (2003)


## NON-FICTION

The Autobiography Box (1999)

Monster: Gay Adventures in American Machismo (2001)

Honorable Bandit: A Walk Across Corsica (2007)

Good in Bed: A Life in Queer Sex, Politics, and Religion (2023)

# GOOD IN BED

## *A Life in Queer Sex, Politics, and Religion*

*by Brian Bouldrey*

# Table of Contents

Copyright ......................................................... 2
Praise for Good in Bed ........................................ 3
Also by Brian Bouldrey .......................................... 4
Dedication ...................................................... 9

EMBEDDED: Memoir ......................................... 11
  1. One Singer to Mourn .................................. 13
  2. The Shock of the Old ................................. 29
  3. Wrestling, Still ....................................... 41
  4. The Dirty Sanchez, and Other Urban Myths .... 49
  5. The Good Pornographer .......................... 53

OTHER PEOPLE'S BEDS: Travel ...................... 73
  6. On Going Back .................................. 75
  7. Faux Amis ........................................ 93
  8. Travels with Charley ............................ 119
  9. Concerning the Spectacular Austerities ......... 131

READING IN BED: Literature ...................... 147
  10. The Duck's Quack Has No Echo ...................... 149
  11. The Terriblest Poet ............................ 155
  12. Leaves of Glass ............................... 163
  13. Phase & Philosophy ........................... 169

BED BUGS: Politics ............................... 173
  14. I, Me, We and the GOP ......................... 175
  15. Drama Queen ................................. 181
  16. The Boy Who Comes to My Readings .......... 191
  17. Finding Freedom ............................. 199

Acknowledgments ................................ 210
About the Author ............................... 213
About ReQueered Tales .......................... 214
More ReQueered Tales .......................... 216
One Last Word ... .............................. 228

*For ...*

Doug P, specifically,

And, ok, also, Richard & Eric, Grant, Rich, Brian S, Todd, Rich, Jeffs E, J, K, S, and W, Elie, Dougs E and M (defer to P, immediately, gentlemen), Robert A (not to be confused with the other 5 Bobs), Johns M and L, Hanks M and H, Jesse, Aidan S, Ralph, Marks D and R, Thom, and Sam, good Sam.

"I believe all your previous lovers should fit on a bus."
— Kathy with a K, *Kids in the Hall*

"Richie, what do you think an XXXXX-rated gay video could possibly show?"

"Restraint," he ventured. "Good taste?"

— Michael Nava, *The Burning Plain*

# EMBEDDED: MEMOIR

"The homeless dudes on Alameda all have legs any runway model would kill for, and sometimes I think of giving them money, but – I don't know, I've got bills to not pay, and drinks to make people buy for me."

— Kris Kidd, *I Can't Feel My Face*

# ONE SINGER TO MOURN

O N THE DEATH OF MY GRANDMOTHER, Mary Bouldrey née
Weber – whom I loved with an unfair but earned prefer-
ence – at the age of 98, I received as my inheritance: her flour
and sugar canisters, an accomplished amateur painting of a
deer in a winter landscape, and a packet of letters she had
squirreled away, letters addressed to her mother, my great
grandmother, Hazel. The letters are from the years 1917 to
1920, the years just after she married her husband John and
before she really started getting busy with raising babies,
which takes away from your letter-writing time.

Besides, she and her many brothers and sisters (I can't
quite get an exact count – at least 8), all becoming adults, all
raised on the same southern Michigan farm, were about as
scattered as they'd ever be or been. One sister, Rita, had run
off to Toledo to do hair and convert to Catholicism; another,
Ila, brain damaged as a result of surviving terrible fever when
she was a toddler, got knocked up by a stranger taking advantage of her disability. Ila got help raising bastard Leo – who
I had known, though I didn't realize he was Uncle Leo the
Bastard – by brothers Charlie and Jack. It doesn't seem beside
the point to say that Rita wrote of Ila's scandal in 1917,

> I feel worse to think it is to be that way, and in plain
> words would much rather hear that she was to be taken

out of this cold world. Of course this seems hard to say but it would only be for the best.

But my family doesn't easily or willingly depart this cold world. We tend to overstay our welcome, and then, suddenly, bid a French Exit to the party of life.

Eight Green children, at least: that's a lot of siblings writing lots of letters. (If genealogy is a relaxing hobby for you, then consider how unrelaxing it might be for a rabbit. I come from a long line of healthy, oversexed farm families.) But above all, the bulk of the letters came from her two other brothers, first Frank, then Emmet, both having enlisted in two different battalions in the army to fight in The Great War.

Of the near-fifty letters and cards, about half of them are written by Frank to Hazel, a can-do mule skinner for Company A of the 328th Machine Gun Battalion – he had a way with an image and he proves my blood connection to me for, despite all our faults, I also come from a long line of impeccable spellers. However, Frank seemed to believe that using punctuation would make it possible for the devil to take his soul, and the effect of his pauselessness is that of a fever dream, swinging from one fact to another without hope for an intake of breath:

Dear Madam and Adam,

Don't let Emmet enlist for he would be a deserter and in time of war a deserter is shot at sunrise you can come here any time but if I was you would wait a while until the buildings are all built I would like to see you all some boys get homesick when they get a letter from home and cry I felt sorry for them and try to cheer them up obey is what the army stands for too bad ma run a nail in her foot I hope she gets along all right I would like to see Bill and Nero [his beloved hunting dogs] – what game did John shoot Sunday well sis I will have to close hoping to hear from you soon tell me all of the news

I know he is blood, too, because he loves to project: here, he speaks of the homesickness of his pals but not his own, and lets his love for the dogs stand, perhaps, for home, and he is of such a hardy stock no bullet, kicking mule, or disease can kill him.

There is a curious pleasure reading these letters to my great grandmother while having none of her own she sent out. It is the pleasure of whodunits, or the pleasure poets must enjoy when translating Sappho's fragments and offering their own imagined words to match the size of thoughts gone missing in the scroll holes. What is clear if not provable to me is that Great Grandma Hazel was a generous writer, a peacemaker, not a gossip but one to confide in; family was important to her and she was, like the rest of the Greens, healthy. That which does not kill the farmer makes him smelly. Though I am three generations from manure, I am predisposed to liking farm folk, perhaps because they have fewer hangups about sex and other bodily functions, having been around all that animal husbandry.

As I read the letters from Frank, and then Emmet and Rita and their mother, as well as a few family friends, and transcribed them, I managed to piece together a story with several curious themes. For example, besides spelling words well and expressing love more effusively towards pets than people, we are also "ungifters" – there must be half a dozen instances in which various items of (farm) value (bags of seed, tire irons, hunting dogs) are given, but then recalled or simply taken back unceremoniously. This is generally accepted as a family trait, and no quarrels arise from the welching. But the story that really rises from a subterranean place among the letters is a thing still true: my family is astonishingly impervious to disease, decay, and death. My great great uncle and his brothers and sisters all discuss, over the three years of letters, friends and neighbors and coworkers and employers who fall to measles, chicken pox, and the grip. In other words, what turned out to be the Spanish Influenza pandemic of 1918. It visited them all, and chose to pass them by.

At one point in late 1918, Uncle Frank's entire platoon

is suddenly in quarantine at a camp in Ohio, and he alone is shipped, without warning, to Camp Custer in Arkansas; though it is not explicit, I feel confident that this was done to protect him from the infected, and for a while, he is the only healthy soldier trained to tend the mule team:

> When I got back to camp Sunday the whole Co was under quarantine I didn't know when I was home that I was coming here [Camp Custer in Little Rock, Arkansas] Monday morning I thought I was going out to drill the Captain called my name off and told us to get ready we left Camp Custer 530 Monday Night and got here Wednesday noon it was some trip I got the best of board and had a good bunk to sleep in I met a tram load of soldiers at St. Louis MO they said that they only got 2 meals a day and it was all canned goods we saw cotton fields cane fields cotton gins coal mines mountains shacks mules goats razor back hogs and negros our nearest town is Little Rock Ark just as soon as we get here 2 boys come down with the measles and we are in a separate squad room quarantined in for 9 days can't go outdoors if any body else is taken sick we will be put longer under quarantine it is muddy here ankle deep and sticks to our feet we had beef steak peas tomatoes gravey butter bread potatoes and coffee for dinner for supper stew beans onions in milk tomatoes pineapple sauce bread and tea and it was good Nelson Coarser was with us but hey took him somewhere else in camp I will write more when I can get out and see something write often

It was called the Spanish Flu because Spain, first, was hit hard by it – but soon after, so was the rest of Europe – and Spain was quite open with their statistics, to both warn and help. Naming the flu after its most honest and well-meaning victim is the very definition of insult to injury, but then there was that vicious joke in the late 80s: "Q: What does GAY stand for? A: 'Got AIDS Yet?'" You are silent for fear of being a scapegoat, but silence, besides equaling death, also isolates you. Shames you. And causes trouble for others. In the early 90s, I wrote a series of "hard-hitting" AIDS advocacy pieces, but under the pseudonym Alec Holland, which you'd know, if you're a comic book geek, is the name of Swamp Thing before he became Swamp Thing. I did it because I wanted to hit hard, but I also did it because I was HIV-positive and didn't want my friends or family to know, and by know, I mean "worry".

"Coming out" of any sort is exhausting. A kid realizing he's gay doesn't just realize he's gay. There are inklings, or perhaps there is the thunderstruck moment, but after that comes the Kübler-Ross journey from anger to denial to fear to that final admission that you like nice sweaters and Cher's endless farewell tours. Coming out can take months, years, even destroy marriages. And when you tell another person you are gay, you have to grab a magazine and wait for them to go through the same steps toward acceptance. And you come out to friends and family one at a time. And you have to wait. For every single person.

And so it goes with carrying a fatal disease. Clearly, I survived, and eventually came out to the world through novels and memoirs that I assumed nobody read. Hurray for me, sure, but I think it's important to say that those who outlive a pandemic do not necessarily live in what Susan Sontag calls "the kingdom of the well".


The second, lethal wave of the Spanish flu came at the tail end of the First World War, when Americans were suddenly conveniently gung ho about killing the Bosch when things were pretty much winding down. An early, weaker version of the virus created some discomfort nearly a year before in the first months of 1918, but killed nearly nobody. The second wave arrived in Boston in September 1918, and spread quickly and without pattern. Even so, every red-blooded American male who could enlist enlisted. Not enlisting meant you were a slacker, which may be why Emmet signed up despite Frank's goading warning. Frank writes that they are packed six to a tent over in France, among people of many lands, some of whom he is racist toward:

> I am glad that they didn't put any Dagos with me when
> a bunch of them talk they sound like a bunch of geese a
> cackling to me I took my laundry to a farmers house the
> woman chewed snuff she chewed the end of a match
> and then dipped the match in the snuff the next time
> I go there I am going to have her give me lessons in
> spitting …

Alfred Crosby, the great historian of the flu epidemic (*America's Forgotten Epidemic*), wrote about the delayed shock most of rural America experienced when they were informed they had experienced a plague. While those in the cities knew full well they were experiencing an epidemic, in a pre-mass-media small-town America, "when you talk to people who lived through it, they think it was just their block *or* just their neighborhood." It was not apparent to the world that there actually *was* a flu epidemic until 1919, when the annual *Farmer's Almanac* noted the life expectancy dropping from 51 years to 39.

We give to war and gunmen in schools and terror attacks and train derailments sensational news headlines, because they come, almost automatically, in neat powerful packages with a beginning, middle and end, because we can see that shape even in the moment of tragedy. Epidemic is such a sprawl, unshapeable, ending not with a bang but with a whimper; you can't map an epidemic as you can zones of war, nor can you write "Here Be Dragons" to warn people away. There is no transformative enlightening message, no silver lining, no troubadour or bard to give prosody to chaos. And when it's finally over, nobody wants to talk about it, nobody wants to do that work of transformation – you are either dead or exhausted. And always isolated with the experience.

It also has its stops and starts, willful or accidental censorships: some things are just better left unsaid. Or, as it lies buried but mentioned in nearly every letter from the years 1917 to 1919,

Nov. 11 1917

Dear Brother & Sister

Received your most welcome letter and was sure glad to hear from you but sorry Hazel has been ill. Hope she is better by this time and are all well at present. Jennarose has had the chicken pox but she wasn't a bit sick with them and it's all over with them now. Harry is busy all the time has lots of work. We have got a nice little place over here.

Jennarose has the chicken pox but she's *just fine*. Reading the lopsided correspondence among the siblings is like watching an in-flight movie with a scene with a plane crash or violent turbulence cut out so as not to disturb passengers, jumping to a scene in which characters are dead and we have no idea how that happened. As if the experience is terrible, but the aftermath perfectly bearable.

One of the few signs of weakness (that is even mentioned among the women and men of that side of the family) is referred to by a family member, speaking of my great great grandmother:

Your mother has given of the best of her life & strength (her youth) to her family & her road has not been smooth but I'm sure it has been a labor of love. I was indeed sorry to hear that so many had come upon her for such a long stay & she with those delicate ankles.

As a seasoned through-hiker, I know I am my great great grandmother's great great grandson. We both have very delicate ankles.

In the mid-90s of San Francisco, I complained bitterly, and even wrote a bitter novel complaining that the sumptuous plenitude of the Boom Economy, with its tech money and high-end restaurants and full employment, made it impossible to get anything done – it was crowded and expensive and full of strangers. What I now realize is that I had become used to living in a relative ghost town, where the sick were too sick to go to the movies or a restaurant – I had them all to myself, and that was, for too much of my experience, normal. Even today, I have a terrible time standing in line.

In Shakespeare's *Henry V*, the Duke of Burgundy tells the victorious Harry – who, for all his risk didn't lose much in the Battle of St. Crispian's Day and is pretty psyched about having a hot new French wife – that France is really suffering after 10,000 able-bodied men died on the battlefield:

> … let it not disgrace me
> If I demand before this royal view,
> … in this best garden of the world,
> Our fertile France, put up her lovely visage.
> Alas, she hath from France too long been chased,
> And all her husbandry doth lie in heaps,
> Corrupting in its own fertility.
> Her vine, the merry cheerer of the heart,
> Unprunèd dies; her hedge even-pleached,
> Like prisoners wildly overgrown with hair,
> Put forth disordered twigs; her fallow leas
> The darnel, hemlock, and rank fumitory
> Doth root upon, while that the coulter rusts
> That should deracinate such savagery.

Nobody is there to manage the land or make the wine, and Shakespeare sees horror there, as survivors of the 1918 epidemic were deeply troubled by movie theaters playing "Mickey" and "Tarzan of the Apes" to nobody, unsold produce in the market, public transport circling the city endlessly and riderless, funerals all day and ambulances all night. Branches crack with unpicked apples. Nothing says death like vigor mortis.

And the survivor feels guilt. My HIV doctor, who also has HIV, doesn't believe in survivor guilt but, having been a great warrior in the epidemic, and instead sees it as a form of PTSD (and lest you tisk at a doctor who ought to heal himself, I remind you of Chekhov's doctor in "The Grasshopper", whose end is icky in any language, though particularly gross in English, as he develops diphtheria by "sucking up the mucus through a pipette from a boy with the disease" – in order to kill himself after he figures out his wife is untrue – that is, that the person he loves is gone). I'm going to let my doctor have PTSD: he went to war, while I served in a sort of civilian work council, and always feel guilty because I think I should have done more, like my doctor. I can see great great uncle Frank watching the infirmary fill, I can sense he feels both overworked by the mules and utterly useless around his sick companions. What can you do, besides pray and skin the mules?

Saint Roch, in the Catholic tradition, a survivor of plague, is the saint you invoke against the plague (hagiography is funny like that: the patron saint of bridges is Nepomuk, a guy who was martyred when they threw him off a bridge). A 14th century mendicant pilgrim from the French foothills of the Pyrenees, who, on his way to Rome, encountered great numbers of people suffering from the bubonic plague. He put down his walking stick and did everything he could to nurse and comfort the sick and dying. Inevitably, he became part of the epidemic and, in order to avoid spreading it to anybody else, went out into the wilderness to die. But God took pity on him and sent, each day, a little dog that brought him bread and licked his wounds until they healed. He is typically seen with the walking stick and drinking gourd, the dog at his feet with a mouthful of bread, and he lifts his robes to point to his rather vaginal-looking bubo wound. Besides being the patron of plague sufferers, he is also the patron of dogs, the falsely accused, and bachelors. Needless to say, I like this guy. And the part of the story where he has been infected, and isolates himself in the woods – that resonates quite a bit for those who survive or outstrip a plague.

In my home, there are at least five devotional statues of St. Roch. I say "at least" because there must be just as many, again, in states of disrepair: his drinking gourd falls off, the little dog comes unglued from his pedestal. One terrible but beloved statue was painted by a palsied nun on the island of Madeira – he looks like he has mascara and has just eaten raw flesh, and his dog is serving him a bagel. Roch inspires me but his leadership may be questionable. Should I, as I have, at least spiritually, gone into the woods to isolate myself from others so as not to give them the plague? Not just the dormant HIV, but the sorrowful memories, the long untransformable story you know will have an unhappy ending – why would I do that to people?

I hear myself in the letters and actions of other survivors. The strange writer Norman Douglas, who survived the Spanish flu and lived far beyond his rights, for example, just kept traveling, for all at home were dead. That's another sorrow of the survivor: it unhomes you. As Paul Fussell describes Douglas' constitution in *Abroad*, "Instead he was raggedy, although he managed to maintain, as Harold Acton recalled, 'the elegance of a Scottish Jacobite in exile.' His constitution was rugged. After a lifetime of excesses – confronted by temptation he always followed his own favorite suggestion, 'Why not, my dear?' – he apparently couldn't die, even at the age of eighty-four, and he finally had to put himself down with an overdose of pills."

The phrase to linger upon is "Scottish Jacobite in exile". Those who live forever find themselves removed from the arc and shape of typical lifespans. It's why Tolkien's elves didn't want to get emotionally involved with mortal men, and why my grandmother, who lost my grandfather in 1978, went on for what I'd call another lifetime, forty years, without considering another man, before she passed at the age of 98. My grandmother, though the eldest of her siblings, outlived all of them, too. "Death always leaves one singer to mourn," wrote Katherine Anne Porter, herself a survivor of the Spanish flu epidemic. Note that this lyrical bromide has been applied to nearly every single horror movie ending ever made.

Just because we are unhomed does not mean there's not work to be done. Great great grandma Green, a tough old bird and a piece of work by any standards, she of the delicate ankles, finds herself doing the laundry for everybody in town as they languish sick in bed:

April 26 1919

Well, Hazel I can see you going to the post office every day looking for a letter from ma & then going home and saying darn it why don't Ma write? But when I tell you all I have done this week you will say no wonder she didn't write – Monday I washed for Georgia Ford & some for her mother in the forenoon. Afternoon I did Libbie's generals, washing three washings one day, Tuesday, I did George Broncing and was going to do my washing and it rained. I had George Eban dress for dinner on Tuesday & Wednesday I had Ina (Ila) Ness come & George for dinner. I did my washing. Georgia Ford and George Broncing and George Eban had the grip. The [somebody's name] came on Tuesday about two o clock & when I ans the ring, Wilda was the one to call she was Rob Chapels she came home with the red measles & had them good & proper she said she wasn't sick But Wednesday I made her stay in bed til five o'clock I was washing and had the doors open I though the fresh air wasn't good for her she has got Pheneralogy I guess you can tell what that word is her face is swelled to beat to faces good spelling what gives her

I remember the year or so, 1992 into 1993, when my partner Jeff was fading – fighting his own good fight but too exhausted to do anything else. I would come home from a long day at work, exhausted, and start up another round of work cooking and cleaning the house and him up. He was not a burden. Nevertheless, I was doing heavy lifting. And the work never quite got done. Just reading about all that laundry in my great great grandmother's letter makes my shoulders ache.

Meanwhile, Uncle Frank had his own tasks. Reading between the unpunctuated lines of his and others' letters, Uncle Frank was, it strikes me, a likable guy – people liked to write to him and send him gifts, and he called out all his seven or so brothers and sisters with fond hellos at least once. But in almost every letter he misses Nero, his beloved hunting dog:

> "keep my pal Nero a hunting every chance you get for I know how he likes it",
>
> "I am glad John likes his new job they told us today that we would get out of quarantine Saturday morning I will be home if nothing more happens I'll bet Nero had a big time over to your place we are 3 weeks behind in our drilling and now we are going to make it up so you see we have some hard work ahead of us we are going to stay in the trenches some night this week",
>
> "Butter Scotch is good to eat but 'Gilberts Chocolates' are lots better. Fido is a good old dog but Nero is a lot better".

The only thing he mentions more often than Nero is, well, people getting sick all around him. And he can do nothing about Nero or sickness.

The Spanish Flu targeted specifically, if not exclusively, young adults between the ages of 20 and 40. Your basic work force, adults with parents still living. While, as the cultural critic Fran Lebowitz pointed out in "On Race and Racism" that "Genocides are like snowflakes. Each one unique, no two alike," the young men from 20 to 40 who fell to AIDS left a similar hole in the population. The world became a desolate landscape of bereft parents, orphans, and widowed spouses. My partner Jeff, who, you will not be surprised to discover, grew up on an Illinois farm that raised polled shorthorns. He had three siblings, and they, along with his parents Joe and Joyce, all had names that began with the letter J. He was buried in 1993 back in his home town in a lovely little cemetery along a river, and twice daily, the Burlington Northern trains roll by and give a lonesome whistle salute. When Joyce, good country people, also lost her husband a few years ago, she had a large family headstone placed for father and son and eventually the rest of them, and specifically ordered that a square hole be chiseled through the stone. Little hinged windows cover the square, and in that hole-in-the-rock space, she rearranges daily little groupings of toy cows, farmers, and tractors. She plays house in the tombstone. "Why weepest thou?" asks the angel to the Marys at Jesus' tomb, by which he means, what are you doing hanging around a cemetery? Because, Joyce would say, playing house in the tombstone, this isn't a cemetery, this is home.

"What is home?" asks Mary Lee Settle in her novel *Celebration*, "The place where you can die." The loss of family is, to me, the loss of home – whether you are shunned by family or if family dies out. You wander the earth like the prodigal son, but there is no place to return to. After a while, you stop looking for home and start looking for a cemetery. It's not that one is eager to get into the grave, but survivor guilt is real, and one begins to do things that might hasten the journey. Katherine Anne Porter's *Pale Horse, Pale Rider* tells the story of a woman who survives the flu epidemic only to find, after a delirious fever dream, that her soldier boyfriend died of it, probably because he caught it from her when caring for her. The last paragraph is worth quoting in full:

> No more war, no more plague, only the dazed silence that follows the ceasing of the heavy guns, noiseless houses with the shades drawn, empty streets, the dead cold light of tomorrow. Now there would be time for everything.

Literary fiction seems the appropriate realm of plague, not because it feels unreal or untrue, but because the wound of the loss of all those people is a wound that never heals, like St. Roch's bubo he always reminds us of in the statuary. Fiction is the place where one can write again and again, with invention and artfulness, the disease and death not an engine – that is, the thing itself – but a spirit, a myth. Half a dozen of William Maxwell's novels and stories (my favorite being

*So Long, See You Tomorrow*) concern a young boy whose mother dies in the 1918 flu epidemic, and the loss remains as acute as the day the cut wounded. You would think the tale would get repetitive, but pain is a pilgrim, and can find a home anywhere.

There is one more letter you need to see. Once Frank got to France, the war was nearly over, and he was just there to bury the dead and marvel at the unpicked grapes among the vineyards. He wrote this:

Savenay, France

February 15, 1919

Dear Sis & Bro

I will write you a few lines to let you know I am still among the living How is everybody at home I hope they are fine and dandy I am a doing guard duty just now I left Paris xmas day and that was a trip that I will always remember as long as I live I would like to get home so I could start work in the spring I mean in March or April I have to have five hundred bucks by first of next January and it is going to make me do some figuring I think eh I can't tell why I have got to have this money just now but just wait a little while and you will see for your self

How is mother I wrote her a few days ago but I haven't got an answer yet Well I must close for this time so good-by

From Your
 Loving Brother

Five hundred dollars was a lot of money back then, as we say. Whether he got it or not is part of a larger mystery, because here's the most important thing to tell you: Frank never came home. Another French Exit. Nobody knows where he went – the best guess was California. With a girl? With a French girl? Efforts were made, but he disappeared, despite an extended loving family he seems to have had no quarrel with, and Nero, faithful Nero, waiting like Ulysses' old hunting dog Argos, keeping himself alive til the day Frank returned. Part of me doesn't blame Uncle Frank. People were going to ask him stories he didn't want to tell.

Since most rural folks didn't, as Crosby points out, know they were living in a pandemic until the new issue of the *Farmer's Almanac* was published, there are few direct references to deadly contagion in my grandmother's letters. Perhaps the most pointed touch upon the trauma is in a letter postmarked from Chicago in February 1919, from Claudine, grandma Hazel's best friend (I think she had a little crush on Uncle Frank), in which she would seem to be referring to a survivor of the flu (not always a good thing, as your lungs would not ever work well again, and convalescence sometimes took years):

> Father's health seems to be picking up. He has had one terrible fight & La La's been very brave.

And traumatic events are often too difficult to write about in a direct, historical way even once, let alone many times. My great grandmother's letters from ground zero of the flu epidemic follow Emily Dickinson's instructions, "Tell all the truth but tell it slant", as "the truth must dazzle gradually or every man be blind." As somebody who makes a life as a writer, sometimes telling tales and sometimes telling truth, it has been a lesson slowly learned that people who do not tell tales, people who, in fact, are often wrapped in silence and self-distancing, are not necessarily storyless. And they are certainly not without feeling. Silence and distance are not indications of a lack of care, but perhaps a clue that one might care too much, that one might not want you to worry. I'm thinking, for example, of Uncle Frank alone with the mules and homesick for his family but only admitting he misses Nero; I'm thinking of Aunt Rita in Toledo wondering whether her own damaged sister might be better off dead, if only to spare Ila the pain of life; I'm thinking of Saint Roch retiring to the woods with his bubos and his memories of plague. And I'm thinking of my old self and my cloak and dagger pseudonyms and omission of infection, and the long journey toward telling this story now – quarantine is what we learned, and quarantine is how we continue to live.

# THE SHOCK OF THE OLD

ADAM GOPNIK, IN A 2018 *New Yorker* essay-review on Edward Lear, the painter and limericist, wrote, "The Victorians, famously puritanical, are also famous for providing the template of modern pornography – the words 'Victorian classic' on a paperback have long meant a dirty book – while on the other side of that earnest, progressive Victorian rationality are the mad leaps of Victorian irrationality." Porn and nonsense change as we change repressions.

In 2017, Northwestern University's Library acquired over 6,000 gay pulp novels, with porno-nonsensical titles like *Roll Call in Sodom*, *Growing Old Disgracefully*, *Home is Where the Hard Is*, and, with less wit but careful distinction, *Hot-Ass Hippie* and *Hot-Assed Hippie*. These books were published anywhere between 1950 and 1993, spotty beginnings leading to a very abrupt end, just like no work of literature.

These books, exciting and shocking for a different time, served, first, a pre-Stonewall readership by offering readers an escape, a coded world where, at least for a few pages, one could leave the self in order to become more himself. After Stonewall, the pulp novels provided a different sort of escape – from AIDS, from small-town life, from the closet, or from a bad marriage. The quality in writing, editing, and production, varies widely: the worst are full of malaprops and utterly egregious production gaffs; in one, the publisher repeated the same chapter over and over, as if they were offering some sort of raunchy Calvino novel; the best were written by literary writers who decided to try their hand at smut for any number of reasons – experiment with genre, honest blue memoir, providing a record of an invisible culture, seeing if a silk purse could be made from a sow's ear.

My first experiences with pornography, besides the *Playboy* I found in my father's briefcase and mistook for a jokebook, were the grocery bags full of Harlequin Romances my grandmother exchanged with her sisters in the 1970s. "Grocery bag" was the unit of measure by which they were purchased and passed, and as a young reader, I was amazed at my grandmother's literary prowess. "Why do you like them so much?" I wanted to know early on, thinking I might like them too. "They're *nice*," was what my grandmother said, and sighed. Picking one up, I found that "nice" meant no surprises, safe as houses, with the occasional frisson of kissing, and, rarely but electrically, a nipple going erect or something in the man's pants pressing against the heroine referred to by the author as his "urgency". The author wasn't lying, I'm not saying that.

Urgency is general, all over America, and rather than waste your time trying to turn my pubescent experiences with porn into a bittersweet memory, I would like to jump to a conclusion: my first library was a library of porn. It was pieced together from things discarded, inherited, and outright stolen. It was catholic, in the catholic sense of the word, because certain pages from the underwear section of the Sears catalogue were allowed to be part. One major source was, coincidentally, the public library itself, where I worked as a page after school and on weekends. I was tasked with emptying the night deposit box by the street, and on Saturday mornings, after the bacchanal of Friday nights in a bored little town, I would clear out rotten Danielle Steele novels, eggs, dog feces, and beer bottles, but this was all made worthwhile at least once a month when somebody "returned" a *Hustler*, or something even more lurid.

My collection of bad romance novels was shared, and not shared, among my friends in a wooden box in the tree fort in the woods, the woods being the speakeasies of rural America, where pot was grown and guns were shot and tippling was tippled. The collection's value was beyond price, overvalued, as anything forbidden or in short supply is, like Soviet samizdat, or Cabbage Patch Dolls. The gay porn and pulp, even rarer, was mine alone, an enigma, wrapped in a sack, kept in a hollowed out chemistry set case, wrapped again in a blanket, and stored in the basement under the winter coats, and it would cause me so much anxiety and self-loathing that I could bear it no more, stuff it all into a lawn trimmings trash bag, carry it into the woods with a shovel, and bury it under a tree like the body of an overdosed prostitute.

My dog hates baths, and when he is in the tub getting scrubbed down, will stick his head far out of the tub as if pretending that his body is some other dog's, not his own as it is scrubbed. I would do the same when reading the porn – this is somebody else's desires, not mine; I am reading this as I would read history, or science fiction. Similarly, they say a criminal will be seized by a particular wooden feeling just before perpetrating a crime. This wooden feeling would occur, but just after, I would feel so distant from myself that the distance had taken me around the world and all the way back home to myself – I was closer to myself than I had ever been. Pulps were an escape from repressed life, and later, an escape from AIDS, but ironically, it was an escape from the self *toward* the self – Frankie Goes to Hollywood, in "Welcome to the Pleasure Dome", chanted, "We're a long way from home/Welcome to the Pleasure dome/ On our way home/Going home where lovers roam." I did not want "away" to be "home".

At night, I would dream of the buried porn out there, the roots of the tree growing around it, turning all those male bodies into fertilizer, dust to dust. In the morning, I would run into the woods with the shovel and dig up my sweethearts. I loved and hated that collection of smut with the same ferocity that I loved and hated myself. Many people get a special high from making up after a fierce fight with a beloved. They love to get into a fight just for the thrill of reuniting. I buried and exhumed the bag of porn three times, just as many times as Heathcliff dug up Catherine in *Wuthering Heights*.

So why would a respectable university exhume, or purchase 6,000 smutty books printed on cheap paper with lurid, usually crummy drawings or photos on the covers? There is so much to say. Think first about writership and readership. Capable, even literary writers slipping into what they might refer to as "erotica"; bad writers given a large audience they don't deserve. People who never even read the newspaper reading whole books; readers who will be reading Proust and Pound on their morning commute slogging through a bad writer's smut. Christopher Isherwood openly admitted he was influenced by pulp. Bruce Benderson, one of the best authors of the pulp novels and one who never concealed his name, wrote a manifesto in 1997, "Toward the New Degeneracy". In it, he deplores the cleaning up or "Disneyfication" of Times Square, and explains that the old Times Square was a place where people from all walks of life – rich, poor, from every race and place, prostitute and john – met and communicated. The pulp novels, too, are a sort of old Times Square of literature.

Throughout the pulps, there are an inordinate number of ways in which the pornography wishes to remain both unapologetic and legitimized, just as gay men did and do. You have never seen so many quotes from the Bible outside of the Bible, philosophical statements (Larry Townsend's *Billy's Club* launches with this wisdom from Pythagoras, "He calls drunkenness an expression identical with ruin"), psychological studies – any way to use reason to justify passion. Samuel Steward, the great tattoo artist professor, established in the 1969 series of Guild books a frontis long essay, sometimes taking up a quarter of the book itself, entitled "The Meaning and Value of Homosexual Underground Literature": "In every culture since the dawn of history, man has inscribed on any surface, flat or round, his sexual feelings. Pornographic liter-ature has never been defined to the satisfaction of any two people. Disagreement is common; a common ground where jurists, lawyers, the public, the artist, the educator can meet does not exist and it never has." Sure. And all the authors of these books were the kind of person who added, "said the actress to the bishop" as an effort to sexualize everything under the sun.

When considering literary worth, there is the tradition of transgression, of carnival or the night journey – and "the demonic mode" – lifting to the level of heroic that which is villainous. In *Blaze of Summer* by Alexander Goodman, each story is capped with an (Im)-Moral: "Don't Cross your Bridg-es before you come to them. OR: To hell with bridges. Don't bother crossing them at all." They also created and broke down literary structures: the "case study", hybrid genres of western, mystery, science fiction, memoir, parody, ballad, and essay. Many of the writers, after the discovery by main-stream media, formed a literary movement called the New Narrative or "Mandarin" movement, and its members include Kevin Killian, Dodie Bellamy, Dennis Cooper, Robert Gluck, and Benderson. Gay pulp was an opportunity for the literary writers to "forget and reclaim what everyday language *is*", as George Orwell described it in "Propaganda and Democ-racy", and though Orwell was not gay, anybody who *falls in love* with his *bedbugs* as he does in *Down and Out in Paris and London*, understands the value of Old Times Square.

Also, these books are artifacts. There is every sort of forbidden subject in forbidden books, what was then illicit sex, but also, all things taboo – drugs, various subcultures, descriptions of parts of cities there was no reason to go to otherwise. There is an honesty that rises from there being little reason for lying: emotional states, cultural criticism about art and politics at the time of the writing, blind items, gossip, maps – the stuff we call today "creative nonfiction". These are "sketches", as if all were hunters and serfs in Tur-genev's *Notes from a Hunter's Album*: character descriptions, situations, occasions, and the hard to define "uninventable detail". These books served as community. There are examples of early crowdsourcing with questionnaires at the back asking what readers wanted more of (Work? Career? Family? Generational? School?). Star Books had personal ads in them in the early 90s, and it would be interesting to know of their veracity and effectiveness. In one of the books, the author described a street-by-street catalogue of Chicago's gay bars and haunts. It is as accurate and complete a map of the city's gay community as can be traced.

Most of all, the stuff was fun, free of importance or reputation. Nothing was at stake, and so anything could happen. It was like cobbling dinner from leftovers in the fridge – a feast, or a famine. We always compliment the host's home cooking, and if it's especially and consistently good and innovative, our highest praise is, "You should open your own restaurant." But once you open a restaurant, there are suddenly fears of health code violations and bad reviews. Out goes the innovation. So it went with gay liberation.

An odd thing to lament, since liberation is a good thing. But repression made us wily, necessity mothered invention. It was the age of Do It Yourself, as well as the age of code. Before the internet helped destroy it and the pulp novel industry, hand-made zines served niche markets with titles like *Diseased Pariah News* for positive men, *Frighten the Horses* for omnisexuals, and two competing zines for gay anarchist skateboarders, *Pavement of Surface* and (my all-time favorite zine title or title of any sort) *Shred of Dignity*. I co-edited a zine, too, *Whispering Campaign*, full of sexual and artistic misfits and loners. What was done at midnight on the law-firm's photocopier is now of great value to collectors and libraries. I get a request at least once a month from somebody offering a pretty penny for the complete run of the zine, but I only have an incomplete set myself.

The late, great poet Thom Gunn, who I dare say was a friend of mine because we both canoodled and corresponded, had in his library a collection of Penguin classics in which he had altered the covers, with their tasteful museum paint-ings, by gluing in naked men cut out of porn magazines. I can never again consider Henry James' *What Maisie Knew* with-out recalling that little girl, and that big man. Mild to his wild, I have in my possession a library of over 150 books that have been signed to me, by the author, with variety, "For Brian, you were great in bed." I have slept with none of them, though I have taken great pleasure with their books in my bed. The pleasure of the word is erotic, whether you like it or not. Even my grandmother knew that. "They're *nice*."

For a few years, I considered it a great honor to be the copyeditor of Cleis Press' *Best Annual Lesbian Erotica* series, for the best judge is a disinterested party. It was my weighty responsibility to clear the spelling mistakes and bad gram-mar (orgasm can be stymied quite easily by a typo), as well as rescue fantasy in its efforts toward reality. "CONTINUITY" I once wrote prudishly on a post-it for the author's consider-ation, "She can't have her hands there, as they were tied up on the previous page." My friend and longtime editor Miriam got her start out of college editing the texts for *Twilight Zone* and a trio of straight porn magazines, *Gallery*, *Fox*, and the high-class *High Society* (any gay man will tell you that "fancy" words and men are code for sex; if you see the silhouette of Mr. Peanut or anybody in a top hat and monocle on a bar sign, you can bet that it's for gays or strippers). "As you probably suspect," she told me, "I did write some fake letters to the editor, but most of them were real, if sometimes embellished. The letters by the boobs fans were always the worst – lots of bad spellings and grammar. But the fetish guys? I never had to do anything to their letters. They were perfect if not lurid."

Not that breast lovers are unintelligent – in the writing about and doing of sex there is always a casual brilliance that has no responsibilities but lifts its laurel'd head every now and then with a perfect portmanteau or metaphor that can get the job done. Certainly, if the brilliance were formal, it would ruin everything.

Well, not everything. I love to laugh at a good bad sentence in these pulp novels. "Ricardo Armory", whoever he was, wrote this dedicatory quote to *Fruit of the Loon* in 1968:

> As Abdul Ben-Gurion writes in *Sex and the Senile Satyr*: "Blessed is he who gets a little." There can be little doubt of this remarkable insight when viewed in the light of the poly-ambivient [sic] dichotomy of the homosexual socio-economic milieu. The following tale, fraught with historic overtones, innuendoes, and outright lies, certainly illustrates this point, among other things.

Or giggle at a dirty limerick. Alexander Goodman, photographer and pulp novelist, assembled the *Gay Psychedelic Sex Book*, each page a collage of men's body parts with a limerick strategically placed where you wish it were not.

> *Because of young Edward's virginity*
> *His friends thought he lacked masculinity*
> *Til he gave them one day*
> *An amazing display*
> *Of his prowess. He's now their divinity.*

Even the great nonsense poet Edward Lear would approve of Goodman's prosody, and – given that he, too, was gay and depressed because of it – content. Goodman's naughty, jaunty rhymes can be suddenly clouded with depression and even troubling horrible truth now and then:

> *There once was a man with a wife*
> *Two kids and a nice, settled life*
> *Then one day he saw*
> *A boy in the raw*
> *And now he knows terror and strife.*

Why did all of this end, almost suddenly in the early 1990s? Desire lines, those paths stamped into the snow when the sidewalk is buried, revealing the way we really desire to go – are evident in the history of pornography, too, for Eros and Thanatos have always held hands under the table. There are several obvious reasons for printed porn's end – the rise of the VHS tape, and then the internet; the liberation created by ACT-UP and Queer Nation, the treatments for HIV that resulted in more "doing" than "describing", and the fact that porn, like all information, wants to be free. But I would offer another reason, another blame: me.

In 1993, my first novel, a gay bildungsroman called *The Genius of Desire*, was published by Ballantine books, part of a tidal wave of LGBTQ+ books picked up by major publishing houses. There had been, for years, fierce supportive publishers like Grove and St. Martin's who published gay literature, but when the ease of repression and the rise of community made it clear that money could be made from queer books, every publisher in New York wanted in. There was a readership, and gay bookstores in major cities to serve the readership, and a disposable income. The home-cooking became a restaurant, and I, for one, feared a health code violation or a bad review, so I backed away from the bold strokes. Soon after, I was asked by Little, Brown to edit the *Best American Gay Fiction* series, and yes, I'll be the judge of that. And in hindsight, I wish I had published a little passage from *Lights Out, Little Hustler* now and then. My compatriots and friends like Michael Lowenthal and Scott Heim raised pulp porn to erotica with fancy titles like *Flesh and the Word* and *Mysterious Skin*. Those are great books, and they endure as much because they were printed on acid-free paper as they do for their complete sentences. What they lack is the potency of a good obscenity, which, as we know, can make grandmothers cry and politicians blink.

Obscenity and sacrilege are two very important and, sorry, natural activities. The nonsense of "Jingle Bells, Batman Smells" matures into all matter of forbidden and nonsensical activity, giving and taking power from those who have and have not. Translating "Jabberwocky" is an obscene idea, and it has been done. When William Blake invited his wife out into the back yard to strip down and read Milton's *Par-*

*adise Lost* nude and aloud, he envisioned it as part of his revolution.

The danger of pornography's power is not in the distortion of reality, but in what distortion can reveal. And the revelation can even surprise and expose the author. Here is another of Alexander Goodman's silly sorrowful limericks:

> *I dream of the boy just for me*
> *Climbing out of my table TV*
> *And allowing my arms*
> *To envelop his charms*
> *Thus refuting the fate meant to be.*

Goodman, by the way, was many things, including the author of the Broadway musical, "Dames at Sea".

While I was living and thinking and making through those years, distracted by the epidemic, and seeing sexuality as mostly a thing of the past or theoretical, I was commissioned to write many gay culture pieces for various magazines and newspapers, usually commemorating annual Pride celebrations. I often considered whether there was such a thing as a gay culture, for could you, I thought, build an entire culture on lust? But as Victor Banis says in his novel The Man from C.A.M.P., "Lust, plain and simple – if lust were ever simple."

While the Age of the Pulps has ended, its sources will never run dry. A new "Victorian classic" rises up as another constraint is imposed. As our nation slips further and further into two camps, each trying to control the other's desires, both finding escape in obscenity and nonsense, for all of us can find ourselves acting as prudishly as the most severe Victorian. While the far and religious right wish to take away the hard-won rights of LGBTQ+ citizens, the left wants to take away certain powers of expression. And so we have alt-right men, supposedly bereft, paying the likes of Steve Bannon and Ann Coulter thousands of dollars for a speaking engagement, if only for the delicious chance to hear their obscene insults and outrageous goadings. Meanwhile, the outraged left gets off creating ridiculous memes in which the President of the United States looks like a giant baby, among other things. After all, "The literature of savage ridicule is the only honorable weapon we have left," as Muriel Spark observed, pert as ever. Pornography and nonsense are expressions of savage ridicule, both of others and ourselves, and their shock value worked then, and now.

# WRESTLING, STILL

TWENTY YEARS AGO, I EDITED a collection of essays written by gay writers born into a wide range of religious traditions: Buddhism, Judaism, Islam, Hinduism – but mostly, a rainbow, if you will, of Christian flavors. It's a collection of arguments called *Wrestling with the Angel: Faith and Religion in the Lives of Gay Men.* The book won me a Lambda Literary Prize, and it's good; I can say that because mostly I didn't write it, I just gathered the right authors. I was putting the book together in 1994 and people were still dying of AIDS. I wrote to several great writers now long gone – Paul Monette wrote the sweetest teaser, telling me he had the best story to give to the book but hadn't the energy to write it. He died a week after writing me the letter. The naked civil servant Quentin Crisp rapped out on a manual typewriter a short letter that looked like a poem:

> *My dear Mr. Brian Bouldrey,*
> *I'm afraid I don't wrestle*
> *With anybody,*
> *Let alone the angels*

> *And so it is with regret*
> *That I must say no*
> *To your admirable project.*
> *With admirable admiration,*
> *Quentin Crisp*

The signature was here signed with a flourishing cursive "2" for a Q and garnished with a debutante's circle instead of a dot on the "i"; I have always sought the company of queers who live up to the prayer Ronald Firbank wrote into *The Flower Beneath the Foot*, "O! help me, heaven, to be decorative and to do right." Crisp was such a decorative, right-doing soul. In that order.

Other authors were not so friendly to the project. The late great anthologist John Preston wrote to me on the back of a postcard, "If anybody were to bother wrestling with THAT angel, I would advise him to take a handful of aspirin and a long nap." I felt put in my place. That story has a rueful ending, for my now good, lovely longtime pal Michael Lowenthal (also a contributor to *Wrestling*) informed me, years after Preston's death, that his shunning of faith and religion was curious. Michael was, after all, John Preston's young protégé, who took over many of Preston's projects after his death from AIDS a year after my book was published. "It's curious," Michael tells me, "because for the last week of his life, he kept a well-thumbed copy of The Book of Common Prayer on his nightstand," proving once again that there are no atheists in foxholes.

Preston's response was the norm, not the exception; when I was assembling *Wrestling with the Angel*, I lost a bit of sleep, egotist that I am, wondering whether a bishop might come to my home and throw candles at me, officially excommunicating me from the Catholic church into which I had been baptized, or whether I'd receive *angry letters* from born agains from around the world. A stoning, a fatwa. Instead, I had a lot of angry people from the gay side of things. Public embarrassment as I stood on the stage with a famous author who mocked any gay attempt to consort with organized religion. Caricatures of me in the gay rags, now cherished mementos among my private papers. How could I be such a hypocrite?, they wanted to know; why would you try to be friends with somebody who hated you? These were real, legitimate concerns. And I get it: it takes real bravery to walk away from somebody who repeatedly abuses you; it seems stupid, even cowardly to try and walk back up to that same abuser. But you wouldn't believe the number of clergy of all sorts who reached out to me and wished the book well, showing that they, too, were and are caught between two polemical worlds. I realized that there were these others, these priests and clergy I always regarded as opponents, but they were on my side, and we were all wrestling with a narrative that didn't work, a meaninglessness, a loss of sense – in fact, the germ of the book was my own surprise, at the death of my great lovely partner Jeff, when I rushed to the church to find something to salvage from that bonfire. I rushed into the church that didn't want me, and I was determined to make them see how little sense, like death itself, that dismissal of me was. That, of course, is the wrestling part. And I wrestle to this day, each day, as if the fight has just begun.

There is a painting in Zurich, the work of Hans Holbein, which uses all his skill as a painter with photo-realist technique, called "The Body of the Dead Christ in the Tomb". There are many episodes in the life of Christ to which artists are drawn, from the Annunciation to the Madonna with Child to Gethsemene to the Crucifixion to the Pietà. This Holbein stands alone – nobody in my knowledge went where Holbein went, nor really has since. It is a painting about six feet long, life-sized, which is part of its horror, and depicts a dead body, one that has been dead for two or three days. It is the body depicted just before the moment all the other painters would prefer to predict; it is the body before the resurrection. Here it is:

The word "grotesque" means "grotto-like"; in the cave. This painting is the definition of grotesque. The mangled corpse, the mouth slack in drawn horror and suffering, the marks and bruises from beatings and nails, that middle finger not extended in the traditional gesture of obscenity, but true obscenity: death by crucifixion, death, the end of meaning. Dostoyevsky's take: "the face has been horribly lacerated by blows, swollen, with terrible, swollen and bloody bruises, the eyes open, the pupils narrow; the large open whites of the eyes gleam with a deathly, glassy sheen."

While the art historian John Rowlands looks past rigor mortis and decay: "Far from conveying despair, [the painting's] message is intended as one of belief, that from the decay of the tomb Christ rose again in glory on the third day," I find it hard to believe – once again, I am wrestling as I have for all my adult life. I'm back at zero, I've made no headway, and I'm exhausted by my own doubt. How could this painting make one believe in the resurrection?

"That painting! Some people might lose their faith by looking at that painting," says Prince Myshkin, *The* eponymous *Idiot* of Dostoyevsky's novel, which is how I first encountered the Holbein ("Oh," said my smart-ass colleague when he saw me carrying that book around to lunch and meetings and other pleasure palaces, "is that your biography?"), and certainly, if it does not shake a Christian's faith in the resurrection, it is by no means a starting place for believing.

And for me, the painting looks clearly like something else I knew quite well: Christ looks like another death from AIDS. Has nobody made this connection before? I've looked in libraries and online, but nothing. My partner Jeff, who died in

1993 – it's the spitting image. The Dead Christ looks like the man I love and loved and all those other men dead from HIV. The bruises like kaposi's sarcoma, the gaunt drawn face and slack downturned mouth. That painting is for me a grenade of past experience made horribly fresh and present. When I look at it, it sends me back to that moment, and I despair, I have to grieve all over again, I have to start all over, I have to do all the work to reflect upon that experience. In Dostoyevsky's *The Idiot*, the picture hangs over the doorway of the house of Rogozhin, The Idiot Myshkin's (whose response to Myshkin's fear about the painting making people lose their faith, is "Yes, I'm losing that, too."). The painting is over the threshold of Rogozhin's house, like a horizontal sentry.

Nobody wants to talk about the AIDS era any more, even and especially the ones who survived it, watched our lovers and friends suffer, die, and get buried, but never rise again, a great game of hide and seek in which nobody ever got found. It was terrifying and hopeless, we survivors are all children who still look into clothes hampers and closets and hope they will suddenly just be there, still hiding. Here: look what I'm doing: making a narrative of something that has no story left to it. There was no romance to AIDS, though I think the foolish young me wanted it to be romantic, just as those who want a messiah are romantics. I loved the romantic stories of the saints, which drew me into their useful mythology the way demigods do in Greek myths – men and gods are inert, but the demigods, not quite of this world or that, little monsters, they get the ball rolling. It was God, then, that I had the hardest part with, way up there, just being, rather than doing.

I keep thinking that I have to restore myself in order to honor those who suffered like the man who is the Dead Christ, if you accept that the dead man in Holbein's painting is the Dead Christ, which is, in itself, a declaration of faith, at least the beginning of one. But what I must instead do is lose myself and dig myself out from the moment. Resurrection, rebirth cannot happen until one dies. Hope dies every time I look at the Holbein. That is the strangest kind of resurrection story.

It's not just this Holbein, by the way. There is a wooden mask of Christ in the Cluny in Paris that is probably part of a whole crucifix, mostly gone and even what is left is in terrible condition, but so was Christ:

There is that horrible aloneness in these two depictions of suffering. But that is where I must now turn to something that is not so direct, not so obvious about the painting. It is about those who view the Dead Christ. Dostoyevsky, again: "But strangely, as one looks at this corpse of a tortured man, a peculiar and interesting question arises: if this is really what the corpse looked like (and it certainly must have looked just like this) when it was seen by all his disciples, his chief future apostles, by the women who followed him and stood by the cross, indeed by all who believed in him and worshipped him, then how could they believe, as they looked at such a corpse, that this martyr would rise from the dead? ... Nature appears as one looks at the painting, in the guise of some enormous implacable and speechless animal, or more nearly ... in the guise of some enormous machine of the most modern devising, which has senselessly seized, smashed to pieces and devoured, dully and without feeling, a great and priceless being."

I nearly want to apologize for quoting Dostoyevsky so extensively, but this is exactly how I feel – and my point is this: it is about how we feel around the Dead Christ, the dead lover, the one who was supposed to make meaning out of the rest of our lives, and in fact did the dead opposite – rendered the world nil. I imagine Holbein, another viewer of his own painting, of his own Dead Christ, working for what were probably hours and days as he put paint little by little to the image. He stared into that abyss for days, dwelling for so long, alone with all hope gone.

Most paintings – most art in general, actually – are in some way meditations, a step away from the raw chaos of life, an artifice, an order that really isn't there. Holbein's Dead Christ is just the opposite. It is an expression of scorching sincerity when I've grown so used to the safety of lyricism and irony. How can I make you see that painful moment in this essay the way Holbein makes you see it in his painting? How can I write this essay that will remind you of that hopeless moment when those boys died, without making you lose hope from here on out?

And yet we need so much to come back to zero, to start the fight over, to wrestle with the angel of death and of life, to remember if only briefly that there didn't seem to be resurrection for anybody, especially ourselves, looking there at that body, without transfiguration or irony or metaphor or lesson or redemption Holbein's is the opposite of lovely and lyric.

And yet: here we are. Proof. Able to live and lose and remember again. It's those just outside the picture that are the engine of hope.

This is all to say I'm still wrestling with all that loss, and I still stand by that book twenty years later. I am sure there are queers who would take new offense at my wish to change organized religion from within, my wish to consort with the enemy. But if you write to me and call me a hypocrite or toady, I will only love your letter, because it will mean you are wrestling, too, and I will have done my job as a writer.

Orwell said, "Journalism is printing what someone else does not want printed; everything else is public relations." *Wrestling with the Angel* was a watershed moment in my life in which I changed my intentions for writing; I used to write to be loved (public relations); now I write to be understood (writing what someone else does not want printed). And to me, the greater, more terrible hypocrisy is our queer demand for absolute respect, while posting Facebook pictures of a slice of pizza being microwaved on top of a Bible because we had "run out of plates". Respect is a two-way street. And all of us are both inside and outside the grotto that seals in the Dead Christ.

# THE DIRTY SANCHEZ, AND OTHER URBAN MYTHS

A FRIEND WHO SPENT HIS YOUTH dancing with a ballet company turned, after the inevitable injury, to choreography. "I wanted to create a dance piece that would include ugly moves," he told me. Football tackles. A body, dragged by a parachute after an unfortunate jump. A waiter tripping with your meal. But it never worked out: once an ugly move was identified, studied, repeated, and transformed on the stage, the ugliness turned to a terrible beauty. Franz Kafka wrote this parable: "Leopards break into the temple and drink to the dregs what is in the sacrificial pitchers; this is repeated over and over again; finally it can be calculated in advance, and it becomes a part of the ceremony."

Kelly, another friend, has a golden retriever named Emma. Emma is a canine manifestation of a ballet dancer, but she has one terrible habit – when you take her to swim in Lake Michigan, she prefers to "do her business" in the lake. Kelly has to wade into the lake with a plastic bag and, in her own version of an ugly move, clumsily scoop doodies up, a soup of poop, lake water and weed. Kelly and I philosophize about this – it can't feel "natural" to defecate into water; the slight pressure in the other direction would feel awkward, especially to such a princess-and-the-pea pup as Emma. But over the years, she has come to prefer crapping in the lake. "You can only hope for floaters," I told Kelly. I had a partner of many years who was Dutch, and the Dutch, being a clean people, are obsessed with fecal matter. As the Eskimos have many words for the different kinds of snow, the Dutch have eight known words for the different qualities of shit. "Keuteltjes", I am told, are ideal: "floaters". Kelly and I, in an attempt to accommodate the leopard in the temple, have given a name to a dog's crapping in Chicago lakewater: "A Hot Michigan Dutchy". This is also the name of the tomato salsa we can annually and give to friends at Christmas.

The "Dirty Sanchez" – the act of adorning a lover's upper lip with a Frito Bandito mustache using the fecal matter from less than clean anal sex – has the visceral shock of an ugly move. Tell a friend about it so you are not so alone with the shock, and then you will not be so shocked. You can only be shocked once when I tell you what a "Strawberry Shortcake" is (punching your partner's nose until it bleeds while coming on them), how to perform a "Cincinnati Bowtie" (insert penis into tracheotomy hole; repeat as necessary) or the "Alabama Hot Pocket" (defecate into a woman's vagina), or that somebody might find pleasure in "The Angry Penguin" (fellating a man while he stands, pants around his ankles, and bringing him near orgasm, then walking away, leaving the fellated man no recourse but to waddle away, pants still down, furious). There are even more elaborate sexual deeds that have perhaps been performed at outdoor rock shows (the "Abe Lincoln": shooting all over an unconscious person's face, trimming their pubic hair, and creating a beard with the pubes and jizz; the "Houdini": while fornicating doggie style, the male pulls out and spits on his partner's back, fooling them into thinking that he has ejaculated, however, when their partner turns around, the man lets loose the true load in his partner's face.

That these acts have names seems dirtier than the acts themselves. I imagine that they are private jokes gone public. In the movie *Klute*, Jane Fonda agrees to perform a "half and half", but we're never quite sure what that is. The imagination runs wild, and the imagination probably has more fun than Jane's john.

I like private jokes. Kelly, after a hard day's work picking up Hot Michigan Dutchies, likes to relax with an Arnold Palmer with Vodka – a "Mrs. Palmer", she calls it. On the other hand, dirty talk during sex seems a bit spendthrift – what we shout at somebody does not always require, necessarily, the articulate breath. Just the gist. Lovemaking, castigating, whining, begging – none of these truly need text, do they? Think of the wingdings used to indicated swear words in comic strips: #&@#$!

But David Byrne once said the only reason he wrote words for his songs was so we could remember the tune more easily. Those are not his exact words, but you get the gist. And you'll probably remember the gist.

Perhaps all these names for outrageous acts of sex are meant to startle memory, fond or otherwise, or to tame the wild. The *Audubon Bird Guide* gives words to birdsong for easy identification. The white-eyed vireo announced, "Quick, give-me-the-rain-check!", the white-throated sparrow laments over "Poor Sam Peabody, Peabody, Peabody" (though up north, he yearns for "Sweet, sweet Canada-Canada-Canada"). The cardinal nesting outside my window dares me to "Party! Party! Party!" Philomel, raped by her brother in law and unable to identify her assailant because he also ripped her tongue out, was transformed into a nightingale. There are no words given to nightingale song, for it is too varied, too virtuoso, and Philomel's is a wordless grief that goes on and on. The difference between the cardinal's song and that of the nightingale is the difference between sex and love.

My partner Jeff, who died fifteen years ago from AIDS, drowned in his own fluids from the weeping of kaposi's sarcoma sores. In his last days, our intimacy was reduced to my examining his body for the advance of these and other opportunistic infections; he trusted me when I ran my fingers over his tender sores, and opened his mouth wide while I placed a long rear-view mirror from an old van into his mouth, to note the purple lesions on the roof of his mouth, the thrush on his tongue. I will not give a name to this long, varied, virtuoso, loving scrutiny of his body, but believe me when I tell you it was an act of both sex and love.

# THE GOOD PORNOGRAPHER

H IS REAL NAME WAS, FLAT-FOOTED and flat, Sam Schad. His stage name, lyrically, Gino Colbert, for he was built for that business they call show, all of it. Gino because who could turn down an authentic Roman dish? Colbert because he loved the great stage actress, Claudette, the one that stopped traffic with her legs in *It Happened One Night*. Gino was known for being a bon vivant, right up to the end, and after a raucous roll in the hay, he was not one to throw you out but make an evening of it – without even asking if I wanted it, he'd lash on an apron (with nothing beneath) and effortlessly chop up and cook out a complex carbonara, searing pancetta and dodging grease spatters on his gold muscled skin while regaling me with his discerning thoughts on various amyl nitrates as if they each had a terroir. He said he was from Toledo and I thought, because he was always a golden brown from head to toe, he meant the one in Spain and complimented him on his impeccable English. He meant the one in Ohio.

We'd gobbled it all naked at his rented Extended Stay kitchen table and he'd tell me stories about growing up in Toledo, Ohio, as if that Toledo were the other Toledo, continental, historical, the source of much great art and event – he'd describe stealing torpedo-sized laughing gas canisters in high school and photographing shy farmboys naked on hay bales and shredding guitars with Lemmy von Motörhead on his yacht. He grew up less than a hundred miles south of me, but he made my Michigan childhood seem prosaic, social-ist-realist gray. He was a Prince of Pleasure, but moreover, he was the Duke of Delight. To fuck and be fucked with not much more than the best poppers from the New Jersey's Cape May coast (flinty, lingering, but hardly any hangover after the finish), to be treated to a huge plate of carbonara and carbs after the workout, to be nearly finished with it when you were then dragged off, back to bed, and in the middle of the second, better, round, to be asked, "While I'm in town, I'm going to see Moby, want me to grab you a ticket?"

Moby! Of course I would. "Nothing crazy, though," he cautioned, and by this he meant no hard drugs. We both agreed a glass of wine and a fat joint made us animal enough. Even these were delights, rather than dark, shitty pleasures. Pleasure, after all, is a word villains use, Ming the Merciless saying it while watching Flash Gordon get executed swilling a French 75 and explaining to his daughter that tears are a sign of weakness.

No, Ming, were merciless-less. Our time was thrilling, acrobatic – Gina Lollabrigida and Tony Curtis taking turns catching each other after doing a triple flip on the trapeze. He was in the moment, unschemed, innocent, performance, sybaritic, all orgasms a reason for prioritizing gratitude – after all: "Thank you, Brian," he would say even before he could catch his breath. My God, I'd think, this dashing porn star is thanking me.

He was, in the sack, a jolly maniac. I loved our sex the way I love black-eyed peas: versatile, dependable, delicious, paired nicely with white Bordeaux, even something a veg-an could love. And like black-eyed peas, no matter how well they clean up for family or company, they never quite lose that hinting whiff of the barnyard. He was six years older than me, but with all that enthusiastic zeal, I swore he was younger than me by that same number of years. He listened to romantic music without irony, he wept to see others' hap-piness. Sometimes, mid-screw, he would slip into directorial mode and suggest I get into a position – hands and knees, Twister-styles, one leg slightly forward, head turned toward the mirror, hands on his ankles as he stood before me on the bed, a bronzed human fireplug, a snub-nosed bulldog with disarming tight curls of blonde-brown hair, a twilight fawn in a twilit glen. After all that marshalling and splaying, I would look up at him and ask, "What's my motivation?" and he and I would fall bouncing to the mattress, laughing so hard we would both weep a little, and that was another communion.

I could have fallen in love with him, but papi was a rolling stone.

When he was gone, he was gone, but when he was here, he gave you his full attention, he gave you everything you wanted and more. In 1987 or so, he got us front box tickets to see Rex Harrison and his namesake, Claudette Colbert, in a play from the 20s, revived, called "Aren't We All?", and our attendance to it seemed to be some scene within the play itself. He said he knew Claudette and after the play, we'd go back and meet her, if I was interested. I was always interested, Sam. Always.

It was just the most minor disappointment for me, when he, at intermission, showed me a note slipped from Claudette Colbert by some usher, apologizing for having to cancel the meeting after the show, but it was a most major disappointment for him. Claudette wrote that Jimmy Stewart and his wife were up from Los Angeles and she had to see them "before we all die", and Sam was so sorry he could not give me that thrill. He wanted me to be perpetually thrilled. Dear Sam, I always was. But to cement the apology, he sent around another porn star from his pool, one I had mentioned having the hots for in some voluptuous, lassitude-slurred conversation after another bang. He was at the tail-end of his time as a performer in the movies in those days, but he was, if anything, born to direct.

When my book on gays and religion, *Wrestling with the Angel*, came out in 1995, and I flew down to Los Angeles to read at the local extension of the great group of bookstores,

A Different Light (all gone, all), he showed up with the entire cast of the smut movie he was filming the next day, "The Matinee Idol". He told me, on several occasions, it was always important to keep the boys occupied the night before, or they'd expend all of their bodies' vital energies. Behind the podium, I recognized Hank Hightower from the "sorry sex" offered to me when Claudette Colbert ghosted us (he waved giddily at me from the rows of chairs at the side of the podium), and Jake Andrews, and Vince Rockland, and that blond bombshell Ken Ryker, who was especially interested in my talk because he was the son of a preacher-man himself. After the reading and my inscribing complimentary copies to the cast, we walked up Hollywood Boulevard to Musso & Frank, that place of shabby splendor, frequented in the past by Marilyn Monroe and Charlie Chaplin and Frank Sinatra. That night, we were the celebrities, and Sam picked up the bill before I could grab it. And I had ordered the ribeye, because it was clearly an evening about thick meat.

From Los Angeles or New York (not New York City, but Rochester, where the porn sausage got made), he would send to me at my place of work his latest opus, at least the flashier of them – the entire "Toilet Tramps" series; "The Dildo Kings"; "Stasha: Portrait of a Swinger"; "Lords of Leather"; "Switch Hitters" inexhaustibly switching 1 through 9; and "Three Brothers", which, more on that in a moment. They always had the return address "Leisure Time", the sort of leisure that might be confused with a subscription to new board games or Omaha grass-fed steaks. These videos always came with a nice letter, often full of gossip about the biz, asking me what I liked and didn't like in the last video he sent.

He hit town one afternoon and we had dinner out, first, because he was starving. "I just filmed seventeen S & M movies, a lot of them bi," he said – it had tired him out. Of course, I perked up. "Really? What are the titles?" He looked at me and laughed and laughed. "How the hell do I know?"

That was the first time I realized that, while he sent me the video projects with bigger budgets and his own scripted storylines, he was beholden to Leisure Time to knock out a lot of janky scenes with less than famous actors, and he had very little control over what was done with these scenes. The thing that was happening with these scenes, it turns out, is that they were randomly grouped together as material for quarter booths in dirty bookstores and low-budget materials that could be recycled over and over again as "new" movies, simply by switching out a couple of the scenes and rearranging the order of events.

This did not always please the actors in those operations, who were paid once for their time but discovered themselves banging away in no less than twelve of the seventeen S&M movies of which Sam did not know their titles. And of course, the company didn't catch hell for this; Sam did. Over the years, as the internet transformed porn and skin flicks with storylines that fell along the wayside, Sam found it increasingly harder to get the big porn names, as they signed exclusive rights with slick studios with horse names like Mustang and Colt and Raging Stallion and (Hung Like a) Clydesdale, or because he did not knowingly tolerate drug use on the set, or because he was a little ahead of his time in light of the niche markets that the online world so easily affords now. He was scrappy, innovative, modular, impulsive, and, for better and for worse, artistic.

Sam always saw his work as a contemporary expression of the burlesque tradition. He was putting on a show, he believed, and everybody loves it when you put on a show. His masterpiece, he wanted me and therefore you to know, was a thing called "Night Moves", which had scenes of hardcore gay porn, but also awkwardy singing, all-male chorus line dancing, stage objects probably borrowed from some theatrical company, men screwing in mascot costumes years before the furries came on the scene, and cinema-scopic extravagance. It was all, all, brilliant, lovingly made, and, sad to say, unclassifiable. The average Joe (and senator and janitor, we are all average Joes when it comes to porn) wants porn to be classifiable. Pornhub has made a fortune on this simple fact.

One of his former stars, who worked for several of the studios and was a great friend of mine even before he entered the world of porn, was one of those actors who did not always benefit from the cut-and-paste hijinks of Leisure Time. His real name is Andy, so I'll just say that if you know porn, you know Andy. Andy is also a person who appreciated the thespian possibilities of porn – he's an excellent actor who was drawn to working with Gino because there were scripts and plots: characters filled out, adventures had, enemies turned friends, friends turned fuck buddies. But Andy also appreciated having a private life, and one way of not having a private life is finding yourself fully exposed on the slipbox that housed a VHS tape. There is Andy, on the cover for that distinguished evergreeen series, "Toilet Tramps".

"I was livid," he told me recently, in a Facebook DM. "I told Gino I specifically did not want my face to show up on any of the boxes. And there I was, sitting on a toilet with nothing on me but a dirty jockstrap. I gave him a piece of my mind – it's why we had a falling out."

That was in the late 1990s, when things were changing, smutwise. Don't you dare Google Andy Toilet Dirty Jockstrap Red, dear reader.

But this story has a sequel. Andy was asked to be in one of those lush productions by Raging Stallion, filmed, in this situation, on location in Hawaii (because you know, we want to look at palm trees and volcanoes and such when watching porn, don't ruin our porn with plot, fools). The studio dashed out an all-expense-paid plane ticket for Andy to get him to Hawaii, but (oh, my, what?) issued the ticket to his nom de porn. Just imagine you, at the airport, going through security (security from 1999, not 2002) and having no governmental identification indicating that your name is Vander/Alessio/ Sean, but you do have one item of identification where your face, etc., is next to the name on the plane ticket.

Andy had a copy of the "Toilet Tramps" slipbox in his luggage, so, quick-witted, he dug it out, showed himself on the cover in nothing but that jockstrap, and then showed his plane ticket name: "Penis DeMilo Stars in Toilet Tramps 12". The security team admitted Andy onto his plane for Hawaii. Yes, Gino, your work outlives you.

Gino was also an excellent correspondent. I'm sure that it had much to do with my being a rising gay writer working for alternative news sources, like my beloved stint at the *San Francisco Bay Guardian*. All his free copies and long hilarious and juicy letters were designed for me to lift his quotes and publish quips about his work. But, before you think he was a schemer, his letters and product were all incidental, not integral. We, representing America before it pruded out, were always networking, both of us: in the sack, over carbonara or ribeyes, playing footsie and so forth under the table.

Arguably, it was Gino's 1998 film "Three Brothers" that was his biggest seller, because, well, he had the three Rockland Brothers of porn, which is a huge turn-on for some people. Not for me, since I am one of three brothers myself, and when I think about doing a flick like this, I throw up a little in my mouth.

And if you are a lover of that fine film, it's been twenty-five years, so you should make yourself ready for the ugly truth: the three brothers of "Three Brothers" are not brothers. Vince Rockland, Hal Rockland, and Shane Rockland might look alike, but they share no DNA but that which was injected into them artificially. This film was to be Sam's masterpiece. He had been working with Vince and Hal for years, and when he found the third lookalike, he penned the convincing screenplay under the name Sam Slam.

As I mentioned, he tried his best to keep the cast of his movies distracted the night before a shoot. He sent me a copy of "Three Brothers" with one of his most eloquent letters, in which he described a terrible dilemma for my friend, the Duke of Delight.

"This movie was made at great expense to my process," he wrote, as Momma Rose would say of Baby June, or Louise. He told me in a beautiful, vivid letter that I own and will save for whoever buys my papers because eventually I will need to fund a handicapable bathroom for my future geriatric self, that he had set the boys up in the same Los Angeles motel where the boys of "The Matinee Idol" had slept after we all celebrated red meat at Musso & Frank in 1995.

As Gino tells it, he took the cast of "Three Brothers" out to dinner, asked them to please save themselves for the movie, but he could not have anticipated the fitful embracing and forsaking situation of he that was Ken Ryker, so-called. The influence of superstar Ryker's ministerial father waxed and waned and waxed again over the 90s, and Ken, if you're reading this, I have nothing but sympathy. For the love of God, I published a book about gays and religion.

Imagine that you are a minister and your son is one of the mighty-mightiest of gay porn stars. That one time, with the football shoulderpads! Sam wrote to me, after he retired that evening in the motel, the cast of "Three Brothers" received a visit from Ken after their fearlesque burlesque leader called lights out, and the Ken in Question was in his on-again phase with religion and dad. Ken's dad came and borned-again the entire cast of "Three Brothers", and when Gino pulled up to the motel first thing in the morning to pick up his cast for filming, the entire strip of rooms he'd rented were abandoned.

Under an ashtray (remember ashtrays?) on a radiator of one of the rooms, some mock-Rockland had nicely scribbled on motel stationery, late 20th century texting: "Dear Sam, We have all been saved by Pastor Ryker (sic). Jesus is Lord! We have given up this life of gay bullshit, and we are now on our new life's mission." Gino didn't have to do too much sleuthing because he knew Ken and his nondenominational upbringing. Gino hopped in his car, drove out to the Ryker church, and found all three Rockland "brothers", as well as Ken Ryker and my personal favorite but don't judge me you gay bitches, Paul Carrigan. "There they were, all painting Ken Ryker's dad's church buses. I stood there watching and waiting for the sun to make everything too hot for them to be Christian. By noon, they were just fine coming back to do 'just one more movie.'"

Such is the life of a strumpet.

And here I ask you, dear reader, where does a paragraph like this go, syntactically, in both time and space, in an appreciation of a porn star fuck buddy with whom I never had a real discussion about AIDS? All around us, our friends and lovers were dying while he and I fucked and huffed and swilled and sucked poppers and dick and spliffs and carbonara and white Bourdeaux, like characters from a French decadent writer such as Jules Barbey d'Aurevilly? For our times together might have been called "At a Dinner of Atheists", even though we were troubled believers begging religions and cultures to let us believe in them when they steadfastly would not believe in us?

I will tell you this, terribly as a confession about a moment of true despair: six weeks after Jeff, my partner, died, Gino and I, with a cadre of his regulars, staged an orgy in the little cottage Jeff and I lived and died in. It was all on me – mostly, I wanted to drive out the terrible silence after Jeff had gone. I am sure Gino had his own silences to deal with.

You don't need to know the gory, sodden details, but overall, that saturnalian night, the dear dog Jeff and I adopted, named Grace, slept well, during the ninesome, for the first time in months. Meanwhile, the sex-bomb smut boys of porn sparked up, caught fire, and burnt down. We fucked in the face of toxic disease and industry, those powers that only wanted to hug us in order to grab our wallet with the reach-around, and for fuck's sake, I was relieved for the lesser rip-off.

Gino Colbert was a unit of measure. How did the 90s begin? How did the 90s end? For me, they have the same answer: the making of the culturally critical porn film pseudo-documentary, *John Wayne Bobbitt Uncut*. How does this appreciation begin and how does it end? An essay I wrote at the height of both our careers. It's worth reminding you that John Wayne Bobbitt was the guy whose wife, in a fit of fury, cut off his penis and drove out onto Washington D.C.'s beltway and tossed it. Miraculously, it was found. Miraculously, it was reattached. People were curious.

In those days, Gino was doing all of his work behind the camera rather than in front of it. I was sending him vintage historical pornography – de Sade, Sacher-Masoch, Krafft-Ebing, Havelock Ellis – while he sends me his latest works – "Lords of Leather", "Tijuana Toilet Tramps", "Men in Blue". The films always come to my office generically wrapped but bearing that giveaway return address, so that the mailroom guy always looks at me out of the corner of his eye when he plops it into my mail bin with the conference schedules and invoices.

One week I got another delivery. This one was different; it was the film every straight guy – and a lot of women – in my office wanted to see: *John Wayne Bobbitt Uncut.*

The day I received my complimentary copy of that X-rated thriller was the same day somebody asked sex advice columnist Isadora about how many straight porn movies were being directed by queers. After all, he was a "herman" (breast) lover and all these women with lovely hermans were being passed over by insensitive camera operators. Isadora responded with her usual well-researched, level-headed advice, and I loosely paraphrase her comments: there's lots of different porn out there, and if you're a herman lover, you might try the films of x, y, and z.

Before going home from the office with my new video, I had to call Gino. "So, were you the director of this thing?" I asked, thinking, oh my god, another friend of mine is about to become a skillionaire.

"No," Gino lamented, "I was just assistant director. Ron Jeremy directed this one." But, he rallied, "I am the sole director of the forthcoming documentary *The Making of 'John Wayne Bobbitt Uncut.'*"

Ron Jeremy, for those living under a rock, was the king of straight porn. Now, of course, he is the king of sexual assault charges, and as of this month in 2023, he has been considered too mentally ill to take to court over the many allegations;

he cannot recognize his own lawyer. But in 1994, he was the king of straight porn. He's appeared in more than a thousand adult movies, from those vintage Super-8 reels right up to the Bobbitt pic and beyond. He's also directed several hundred movies. He has two bachelor of arts degrees – in theater and in education – and held a New York teacher's license. He's no dummy. Plus, he has a very large penis.

When he released *John Wayne Bobbitt Uncut*, Jeremy held a benefit screening for Children of the Night, a shelter for runaway teens – one of George Bush senior's peculiar but perfectly valid points of light in the burgeoning American galaxy of philanthropy and yet another reason why this skin flick is a social document.

How did *Uncut* come to be made? According to Gino, it seems that in their salad days John and Lorena enjoyed Jeremy's porn channel immensely. After the brouhaha, Bobbitt spotted his idol in some public setting and asked for an autograph. Jeremy asked Bobbitt to do a cameo in another movie he was making. Bobbitt declined. Then he called Jeremy back and suggested that they do a whole movie to "show them what I've got."

They had to move fast. A deal was made on a Monday and the shooting began the Wednesday following. "We had to make it quickly," Gino explained. "We were afraid John would have to do time in jail, so we got him through the movie on an eight-day shoot."

What was it like to work with Ron Jeremy in the mid-90s? "He sleeps on the set. He won't bathe. He doesn't change his clothes – same filthy, stained underwear day after day. That's how he was in 1988, and that's how he was on the Bobbitt set. Some people just don't change."

I asked Gino if he'd get in trouble if I quoted him on that. "Oh no, he's proud of it. It's funny to him. Only a straight guy would think his filthy underwear is a plus."

How do Jeremy's actresses respond to this director? Well, the girl on whom he performs cunnilingus in *Uncut*'s orgy scene reported started screaming, "I do not want to *work* with *you* – I came here to be eaten by John!" and stormed off the set. Gino calmed her down, explained the idea of droit du seigneur, and coaxed her back onto the soundstage. "Just let him eat you," he cooed.

Later, actress Letha Weapons puked after Jeremy licked her hermans.

"It's one big party for Ron, which just adds to the disorganization," said Gino. "He invites his rocker buddies onto the set," which accounts for *Uncut*'s memorable sound track by Lemmy Von Motörhead. This is one thing a homo would never do: let his buddies make cameo appearances in his movies.

I have an old man's fondness for the physicality of the VHS setup; there was something intimate about slipping the tape into the box, how it took a little push but then grabbed it in its own gears and pulled it all the way in. I think about this whenever I buy a candy bar from the vending machine in the university library, me reaching in through that slotted door at the bottom, it resisting, then accepting. And now the tape is whirring to life, and now the screen is filled with clearing static.

Here's the setup of *John Wayne Bobbitt Uncut*: It's a docudrama of what happened to John before, during, and after his tangle with the not-guilty-by-reason-of-insanity Lorena. John plays himself, the rest are merely actors. Kind of like the made-for-TV movie in which Joan Rivers and her daughter play themselves, thus making it an "authorized biography" rather than an unauthorized one. So of course the woman playing Lorena Bobbitt is a mean girl from hell. Only she has the most bodacious hermans you have ever seen.

What a tough role to play! To be simultaneously voraciously murderous and irresistibly voluptuous. Why, only the greats have attempted such roles: Salome after John the Baptist, Judith caressing General Holofernes, Kundry wooing Parsifal. Veronica Brazil is a canny Lorena Bobbitt, and she has a lot of emoting to do. John narrates, John copulates, but Veronica *acts*. We see her dragged to an officer's club, where she meets her future husband. Scenes of romance, poetry in the park. They marry. And then she stops putting out. Gratuitous scene with her stealing money from the till at her manicurist job.

Meanwhile John turns to strip joints for his sexual outlet, but ends up coming home late and unsatisfied and demands – ever so gently – nooky from Lorena. Finally she's had enough. She flashes the kitchen knife, she reaches beneath the covers, and yikes! Fade to black. This is a porno movie, not a slasher pic.

Next we see her throwing the penis from the car window. A homeless guy spots it and thanks heaven it's not his penis. Two policemen report how they found the penis. A doctor tells how he reattached the penis.

Now, these guys, these extras, they look vaguely familiar to me. That one policeman – who is that? They're gay male porn stars with their clothes on (that's why it took me a minute): Rod Garetto, Jared Clark, Mitch Rabida. This is when I suddenly got the sense that maybe that herman-loving guy in "Ask Isadora" was right.

And up to this point, except for the strip show, this whole production could have passed as a gay porn movie. Why do I think so? Queers are so good at scripting, at tasteful sets, at *fantasy*. It's all about acting. Queers have been acting (acting straight, acting tough) since the day they discovered they were queers. Queers know all about believability.

They also know a lot about taking decent photographs of a man's penis. So I'll bet even the next scene – despite the female lead's voracious mouth, huge kajoobies, and extended clitoris – was advised and created by guys like Gino. Because this is the scene, on a well-built hospital-room set, where John Wayne Bobbitt, wearing nothing but one of those peeka-boo hospital gowns is miraculously, uh, resuscitated on his bed by a very caring nurse.

This is the scene we've all been waiting for. This is the scene where we want to see *it*. The reattached penis, that miracle of modern medicine. And who, even the guy in "Ask Isadora", would want to put the filming of that revealed member into the hands of just any moviemaker, even if it is that master of erotic celluloid, Ron Jeremy? No, you want somebody who *loves* penises. You want somebody who's not afraid to get close, get curious.

It is my opinion that this scene is at the center of not only the aforementioned movie, but American culture in general. Here, as Nurse Julie mounts the (yes!) erect Frankensteiny penis (that's not fair; it's quite evident in this scene that the real-life surgeons did a very good job) – here are all of our hang-ups about sex, medicine, the private life made public, popular taste, litigation, and the thinning line between fact and fiction.

The scene reveals our hang-ups because it marks a cross-roads: Even the most puritanical American is at least a little interested in John Wayne Bobbitt's plight. Every minute of Bobbitt's story had been combed over by the media; he had been turned into a sounding board for all the fears we have about the failures and successes of our modern world. And *Uncut* takes some time to capture all that – *and* get you hot. Thus does a porno film become a piece of metamedia.

For how do we legitimize the curious heterosexual male's desire to see what everybody else wants to see, a guy's dick, without making him feel, well, like those guys who like other guys' dicks? What do you do? You throw in a couple of be-boobed nurses and make it into a documentary-style scene. Just the facts, ma'am. But a couple of naked nurses will do nicely, too.

Here is a scene that is simultaneously erotic, clinical, and sensational. Bobbitt has been shaved and Naired down, like a gay male porn star, to highlight his well-muscled body and to take away any distractions from his erect schlong. The camera is set at hospital bed level, and as Julie takes the object of our desire, the lens pans slowly, revealingly, like Sherlock Holmes's magnifying glass. The scene intensifies. Yes! It does get erect! Yes, it is able to penetrate! Yes, oh my god, it does ejaculate!

And weren't those some nice hermans, dude?

But eventually *Uncut* becomes, quite apparently, a hetero flick. When exactly do the straight guys take over in *John Wayne Bobbitt Uncut*? Let me put it this way: Do you know those multicolored baggy drawstring pants that wacky frat-boy types wear around? Do you know what us gay guys call those? We call them "straight-boy pants." Because no self-respecting homosexual would get caught dead in a pair of them. What's at stake here is good taste, even in a milieu of bad taste. If you've never seen a gay porno flick, check one out. If the sex seems disgusting, you'll at least be impressed by the décor and the view.

You can see the exact point at which Gino left Ron Jeremy's set: after the premiere exposition of the penis in the hospital room. Our work, the queers seem to say, is done. Have at it ladies. "If it were my movie," Gino told me. "I'd've shot it from the hospital bed scene looking backward." Only a homo would use a flashback technique in a porno film.

The ladies are lovely, the sex is hot, but alas, the last hour of this full-length film is the triumph of goombah straight-guy taste. Out comes the ugly furniture, the peppermint schnapps, the paparazzi, the jokes that somehow fall flat.

Ron Jeremy must be given some credit here, before I sound like the movie's not worth watching after the unveiling. The guy in "Ask Isadora" is advised to check this movie out, because there's a herd of hermans on the loose. But John seems, at times, overwhelmed by them.

As you may or may not know (being an inquiring mind can be exhausting), Bobbitt is continually being chased by the large-hermaned version of the Eumenides. After the film came out, one of *Uncut*'s costars, Tiffany Lords, claimed that Bobbitt got her pregnant during the filming of this movie. *If* that's true, then the film is an even more complete document of Bobbitt's life.

It's probably not true. Gino doesn't believe it. But hey, "*Se non è vero*," say the Italians, "*è ben trovato*." If it's not true, it ought to be.

Gino was very impressed with Bobbitt's good behavior.

"John was a pro," he said. "He functioned very well with all the women – except for one." That would be Veronica Brazil, who was made up very effectively to look *exactly* like Lorena. It freaked John out and he failed to achieve, uh, liftoff with Brazil. Brazil was so incensed she used her disappointment to become the best Lorena Bobbitt ever portrayed in what is, sadly, the "lost footage" – the cut, as it were, from *Uncut*.

What is the lost footage? A scene in which Rod Garetto, gay porn star extraordinaire (am I making my case?), intercoursed the bejesus out of "Lorena" in a scene so hot that all the other actors fought to watch through the peephole of this closed-door set. "It was the sexiest scene in the film," said Gino. "You truly believed Brazil knew from experience, after her bad experience in bed with Bobbitt, when she yelled, 'My husband never fucked me like this!'"

Why was the scene cut? Because, upon scrutiny of the court trial records, Lorena Bobbitt the Real made it clear that she had *never* cheated on John Bobbitt, even once. Jeremy feared that she might file suit if they showed a scene of Lorena performing extramarital sex. Which just goes to show how all concerned believe that they'd not only made a skin flick, they'd made a *document*. And twenty-five years later, it would seem that all porn is document, an archive of desire.

Before its release, *Uncut* had 100,000 units on preorder. After being out for only a few weeks, sales hit a million. Bobbitt found his niche. He moved to Vegas. He became a stripper in Florida and elsewhere. He was master of ceremonies at a drag queen Lorena Bobbitt lookalike contest.

I'm not making this up, you know.

I like porn the way I like *Beavis and Butthead*, detective novels, and opera: They are rarefied, histrionic, unnatural; they delight me like those ancient Egyptian figures in the tombs of the pharaohs, with giant heads and tiny bodies, do. And yet in their exaggerated state, all these things reveal so much about us. There's so little at stake, so few demands on being accurate, that the distorted representations show us our most vulnerable, truest places. They show us what we desire. If it's not true, it ought to be.

In this instance we want to see a penis that's been lopped off and sewn back on. We want to see the unluckiest man in the world get lucky. We want to see whether there's life after death.

And isn't this a case of life after death? There's something weird, something eerie – like the story of Lazarus dying and then coming back from the grave – about having a part of yourself, any part of yourself, severed from the rest of your body, and then having it be fully functional after it's been sewn back on. John Wayne Bobbitt, bless his heart, is fully functional.

And yet, and yet. There's a ghost of that penis running around, haunting the Beltway, showing up in our worst nightmares and on the lowest-class talk shows. "John says he sometimes calls Lorena, but she hangs up or doesn't return his calls," Gino said. "Seeing the way he was around Veronica Brazil all made up like Lorena, I can see he still has a thing for her." Imagine, like I do, the ghost penis pining for the past, for Lorena, for a more complete life before the fall. This is longing, desire without an object.

*John Wayne Bobbitt Uncut* represents that longing, too; it resides in that place where all our general mass desires come together. And where gays and straights come together, showing us that we have similar sorts of enthusiasm. We're not all that different. So we should all be looking around for the even deeper probing of gay-boy Gino's *The Making of "John Wayne Bobbitt Uncut."*

But that never happened.

The last time I saw Sam in the flesh was at the gay porn awards, the Grabbys, in Chicago in 2006. It was on the same stage where I first saw Pee-Wee Herman perform 25 years before that, and I say this because these two events neatly bookmark my innocence and experience.

In 2006, however, I was at the beginning of the worst part of my life, because I had come across enhancements that were not white Bordeaux, or amyl nitrate. I came to those gay film awards with my newly anointed 12-step sponsor and he didn't know it, but I had just relapsed the day before and I was a ragamuffin who had walked into an open door and so I had a head injury heading into a room full of gay men who loved sex and porn. I had starved myself on meth. My clothes hung off me like something from a T.S. Eliot poem describing a scarecrow. I was unrecognizable, even to me. I sat at a cabaret-style table, while strapping porn guys paraded through the space, and I had welded sex, psychologically, with drugs, and so I was not happy to see any of this.

And there, weaving among those little candle-lit tables, was my old fuck-bud Gino – I hadn't talked to him for at least eight years, and why would he even know that I had moved to Chicago? To my scarecrow, he had become a charter member of the Moscow State Clean Plate Club. Chi Chi La Rue, his brash rival, escorted Gino toward the front stage and I, buzzing and ashamed, half-heartedly touched his sleeve hoping he'd see the old me – but something else was going on with him – he was in his own hellhole, frowning, ungolden, spangled with pimples. Like any addict, I figured him for an addict. But that was not the case.

Toilet Tramp Andy told me that in Sam's last years, he was no longer able to make his way in that business he called show. He muddled through by waiting tables in a fancy Italian restaurant in New York City, and I know he had to field all the complaints about somebody else's carbonara, assuring the discontents that it was made with love. Apparently, my friend Sam had put on so much weight, he had a heart condition, or something more complicated than that – life at the cusp of sixty years is perhaps more problematic than anything before or after.

I write this now at the age he was when his body was found, almost two weeks after the event, dead in his own bed, from apparent massive cardiac arrest. I would rather say that he died of a broken heart, because dammit, that's what it was. I am sorry I did not remain close to Sam in the 21st century. I think we could have helped each other out. For all our naughtiness, our friendship was good, clean fun. I'll only remember him the way I first saw him walking out of the steam room of the Tenderloin YMCA, muscled and smooth and bursting with life like a buff porpoise. "His delights were dolphin-like," Cleopatra declaims through Shakespeare, remembering her middle-aged love for Antony, now dead. "They showed his back above the element they lived in. In his livery walked crowns and crownets. Realms and islands were as plates dropped from his pocket."

That's how he was, friends and fans. Remember those years when you gamboled and dove, aware of your body's blow-hole. Let us all toast those years when we only came up for a moment, for air, for carbonara, in order to dive down deep again.

# OTHER PEOPLE'S BEDS: TRAVEL

"Traveling: it leaves you speechless, then turns you into a storyteller."

– Ibn Battuta

# ON GOING BACK

"Then I returned, and I saw vanity under the sun."

*– Ecclesiastes 4:7*

## 1.

ANTHONY, MY PARTNER OF MANY years and now the butt of all my ex-boyfriend jokes, is the best traveler I know. He is miserable at home, but on the road – whoopee! I remember once looking out the window of a secluded Tuscan villa within minutes of our arrival and, hanging in the lintel like a younger, hairier Helena Bonham-Carter in a tasteful, saucy Merchant-Ivory film, I sighed, "I want to come back to this place already."

But Anthony shook his head: "The world is like a giant lawn, and it is my goal to mow every corner of it."

The first time my father let me mow the lawn, it was fun. Ever after, he never could pay me enough to do that kind of work. And you'd think a fairly bright guy could extrapolate from this life-lesson and realize Anthony was right: he did not say "The world is like a giant lawn, and it is my goal to mow every corner of it twice." But I did not extrapolate, and I did mow twice. Once.

The first time I walked to the pilgrim shrine of Santiago de Compostela in 1996, I met several lifelong friends, and among them was Petra, a German girl who has been my backpack mate for a decade now: together, we have mown Corsica, Hungary, Austria, and Canada. On first meeting, what had deeply impressed me, being a boy and therefore being competitive, is that Petra had made the pilgrimage to Santiago twice, two years in a row. This was her second time down the road. The first day I encountered her, we both, separately, chose to part from our companions to walk alone on a detour that added two miles to the day's walking, with only a remote Knights Templar church as a reward. We walked alone, together. We had the trail to ourselves, and we got to be fast friends, fast.

"Is it easier to walk this way a second time?" I asked her then, thinking I already knew the answer: knowing where you're going, you know what stones will trip you, from what window they will throw boiling water on the hobos.

"No, it is much more difficult!" she said. "In your mind, you know what the next town looks like, and in your imagination, you are already there." I imagined her imagination, the map of the world collapsing, time taken out of the equation, destination the only goal for each day. Think of the way you're a character in a play scripted to be slapped, and you telegraph a wince before the actual slapping.

So when Jean-Philippe, another, other fellow pilgrim, suggested that we make a second trip down the road to Santiago six years later, I decided that Petra's wise words did not apply, because six years had passed, during which time I had, as it were, forgotten my lines and when to wince; also I would be doubling the time, mileage, and misadventure by starting at one of the traditional starting places in central France: Vézelay. What had taken a little over a month to execute the first time would take two months this time, and half the road would be new.

A couple of weeks into our walk from Vézelay, we were directed by our makeshift guidebook (a folder full of photocopied maps and directions created by "Les Amis du Chemin de St-Jacques") to stay at the convent of Ste. Marie de Frugie, in La Coquille, somewhere in the dewdropped Dordogne. Blackberry brambles almost ready to fruit, choke cherries almost gone by. Cumulus clouds in orderly fleecy rows, dragging the occasional thunderhead, raining on its own parade. Rain is delicious as long as it doesn't touch you.

I was taken, all along this road, with the way religious and daily life are never separated in countries in which everybody is pretty much of the same faith (and by countries I mean France and Spain and Italy.) (And by faith I mean Catholicism.). Because of this, there were odd juxtapositions, even contradictions, at least to somebody like me, the sacred and the profane not only next to each other, but informing each other: a big crucifix at the edge of a village overlooking a great pile of junked, rusty, abandoned cars; a restaurant's piped-in muzak featured "Ave Maria"; a basketball hoop installed in one church door, and in another, the goals for soccer established at the door of a modestly-sized cathedral. From my own small bed in our cell Ste. Marie – for that's what it was – I noticed a little disposable air freshener beneath the crucifix. Jean-Philippe had tied one end of his laundry line to Jesus' hand, the other to a nail in the windowsill.

This convent was decidedly old-fashioned, full of ill-lit massive statuary of obscure saints, impassive as cigar-store Indians. Next to my head in bed, St. Francis watched over me, his arms crossed with little white birds in his tonsure; beasts gamboled at his feet. This was just fine, until I woke up in the middle of the night and felt the profound disorientation I feel when spending the night in an entirely different place every single night, and saw the looming shadow of My Protector, and nearly hit my head on his wooden head.

The evening before the concussion, the nuns insisted we join them for dinner. Since the town had no restaurants, we decided to accept. We ended up eating in a large hall lit by stained glass windows of perhaps more secular subjects, meaning geometric shapes, so that Jean-Philippe was bathed in the light of a red square while he ate his blue omelet and I kept being startled. We were joining a well-watched group of two dozen wayward boys, troublemakers set on the straight and narrow with a cadre of tough-looking priests (hellion-to-priest ratio roughly 3-to-1) and led by nothing less than the Bishop of this region! A bishop, I wondered at the introduction. This guy was young, younger than me by ten years at least, and I wondered what I had done with my life; somebody ought to knock some ambition into me. The bishop had to wear the simple black but gave vent to his vanity by fiddling with his tonsure. He'd taken great care with his mustachios and with sideburns that ended in complimented points; he had even experimented with a "fade". If I had had the Gall vocabulary, I might have complimented him on his "fade". What, I wondered as I dug into my own geometric cobalt-colored omelet, was the French word for "fade"?

"Where will you go next?" the Bishop asked us, to make awkward dinner conversation.

Jean-Philippe and I gave each other a conspiratorial grin. "Thiviers," he answered for both of us. There is a reason that we knew the word was loaded, a reason I will give in a moment. We enjoyed an outburst of froggy braying from two or three of the bad boys, quickly silenced by one of the priests.

We knew the Bishop would react somehow – inhale, exhale, bug out or narrow his eyes, smile, not smile. He squirmed a little, and said what he knew he would say, "Well, but I advise you, do not go to the monastery called 'Partage'."

We had heard of the Monastery Partage in Thiviers from our various evening hosts for more than a week. The name Thiviers was anathema. We were very excited. But we never heard the same explanation for The Thiviers Evil more than once, though the direness of the offense grew more colorful the closer we drew. In Limoges, the perceived problem was comical: the Thiviers monks were guilty of giving bad haircuts. Someone else told us they were rejecting the word of God. According to the Périgordians, the monastery of Thiviers was practicing medicine without a license ("Do not show them your horrible pilgrim feet, monsieur!"). The Bishop of Ste. Marie now said, "There is a Vietnamese abbot there, and he is performing exorcisms. It is a very strange business."

Vietnamese Exorcisms! That was a new one!

Jean-Philippe leaned in to me and took a chance that the Bishop would not understand his English. "They take Visa and Mastercard."

The next morning, we were not allowed to leave le Frugie, to continue our walk among the brown cows and spools of hay of the Périgord without first taking mass. *Pas de problème*, of course, since they never charged us a single euro, and they had served us the omelet dinner and promised an omelet breakfast. As the priest entered (somebody we hadn't seen the day before), he opened the mass. In Latin.

How odd, I thought, knowing from the catechism that Vatican II had commanded all masses be performed in the local language. Isn't this Latin forbidden? Well, of course it was. We had stumbled into a bunch of renegade Catholics who followed a fellow named Lefebvre, who wants nothing to do with reform. Jean-Philippe was no help; he is an agnostic (when I lit a candle for my favorite saint, Saint Roch, he watched me drop two euros into a canister and said, "A beer also costs two euros. You feel better after a prayer, but I feel better after a beer."). I was able to follow the mass without much problem because of all the requiems I had heard by Verdi, Mozart, Fauré, what have you (and by "what have you", I am afraid I mean the Original Cast Recording of *Evita*, in the opening funeral mass). The real challenge was going down to my knees to take the communion, feeling the sacrifice in my sore feet and legs.

Renegades! When everybody is of the same faith, when there is no separation of church and state, people look for ways to differentiate themselves. This explained a lot of things at le Frugie: the youthfulness of the visiting Bishop, the great dusty library, and the chapel there, glutted with too many candelabras and fading gladiolas, a reliquary or five, mismatched sconces, more wooden saints. Jean-Philippe leaned over, right during the Apostle's Creed, and pointed out a note on the door beside us: *Cost of a marriage: 92 euros. Cost of a funeral: 92 euros.* "Coincidence?" he asked, using the French pronunciation.

After good renegade coffee, we were happy to be on the road again. At the door of the convent, I admired another of the impassive statues, this time, of Ste. Matthilde. She had a plate in one hand, which may have been used for calling cards at some point, but now, as we could see with a few centimes of a euro scattered casually as "seed donation", we knew we were expected to give a little bit. I liked her, and so did Jean-Philippe, for she seemed to be lifting her skirt for us with her free hand.

"Who is Matthilde the patron for?" Jean-Philippe asked me, like I'm some kind of authority.

"Perhaps for you," I suggest, since she'd offered her political leaning, *sans-culottes*. "I will drink a beer for her," he affirmed, but he and I both dropped five euros onto the plate. We looked into our makeshift guide. The advice about the Monastery Partage: avoid it, because of "the legal proceedings". Nothing more. It was as if, every day, as they warned us off the monastery, the invitation were renewed for us. Perhaps I would get exorcised of all my inner demons!

# 3.

I HAD BEEN WARNED, TOO, ABOUT the region of land beyond Thiviers called Les Landes. Friends had motorcycled through it. A flat, sandy, piney region that looked as if it might be peopled by beaver traders, it was planted at the command of Napoleon with forests and forests of regularly spaced pine trees. "You'll die of boredom," my cycle hog friends told me, since they had nearly done so, spacing out looking at spaced trees until the regularity of the road nearly brought them to crash. But Les Landes was a sweet respite for a walker used to getting disoriented when a road curves even slightly, and when a small hillock can create a great effort. Under the shade of the infinite pines, with the soft needles pillowing an even softer sandy ground, we drifted through that region as if in a dream – the one where the corridor stretches out forever and forever before you.

Travel by foot differs from travel by any vehicle. You move, but you seem to move in "real time". And yet you feel as if you are making great haste: There is a funny little footnote in the 1895 edition of *Uncle Remus: His Songs and Sayings*, written by Joel Chandler Harris himself: "It may be interesting to note here that in all probability the word 'skedaddle,' about which there was some controversy during the war, came from the Virginia negro's use of 'skaddle,' which is a corruption of 'scatter.' The matter, however, is hardly worth referring to." Things hardly worth referring to seem important when walking, and vice versa; footnotes become keynotes, and vice versa. Scattering and skedaddling, from the same source, pull away from each other, one sapping energy, the other, a source. All sorts of things seem contrary to the way you have always perceived them. It's like finding out a person you thought was straight is actually gay.

It may be that walking helps make other fine distinctions you could never perceive while moving so quickly through a noisy world. I have discovered that the difference between being alone and being lonely is big, and only comes to you when walking, which one must do alone, even if you are with a dozen other people. The fact is, I never learned how to be alone until I grew older. There's something in our culture (and by our culture, I mean gay culture) that equates "alone" to "failure". And while gay men seem lonely, that's not the same as alone. After I worked all this out while tromping down the long sandy corridor of Les Landes, I began to have a bad feeling about walking over the same trail twice, which I would soon do, once I crossed the Pyrenees into Spain. Going a second time meant I was not only not lonely, but not alone.

Anyway. Somewhere along the piney corridor of Les Landes (that sandy soil makes hydrangeas red, and cornflowers purple), a shiny Renault zipped past us on a stretch of asphalt we had to pass along. It slowed, then stopped. I had a moment's panic. Though I'd been buoyant believing I had thoroughly skedaddled, I couldn't really run quickly if this were foul play, not with a backpack pulling down on me. But as with any suspected instrument of foul play, the Renault turned out to be a beneficence, manned by a priest in a white cassock, a Père Blancs, as Jean-Philippe explained to me as he approached us, his hazards flashing, his car door agog. He spoke to Jean-Philippe as if he knew I wouldn't speak a word of his French. "I see you are going to St. Jacques," he said. You can always tell a pilgrim by the cockleshell pinned to his backpack.

We nodded – you caught us.

"Have you had the communion yet today?"

Hell, we hadn't had communion in weeks, not since the renegade convent of Ste. Marie de Frugie. So we said no. And right there along the side of the road, with other Renaults whizzing by and people staring at us, on our knees, backpacks still over our shoulders, this priest gave a mini-mass (not in Latin this time but in inscrutable French) and offered us communion.

It may seem funny, but this was one of my fondest, most incongruous memories of that second pilgrimage. I wish I could go back and find that stretch of unimportant freeway where I received communion by an anonymous priest. But that's a foolish wish, isn't it? The desire to go back is the desire to be an expert, a master, to go native – and that isn't even possible in the place where I live and work. I want to make all those incongruities and dichotomies smooth, or hold them together with some sort of mental glue.

# 4.

ONCE JEAN-PHILIPPE AND I HAD crossed the Pyrenees into Spain, we were on familiar terrain, and this was, as I suspected, not a good thing. There was, first of all, the impulse to tell all those people (and by other people, I mean fellow pilgrims) to "get off my property", though we were the ones tramping through the back yards of villagers every day. Jean-Philippe and I were so much our own little unit that it was hard to meet us, if you were a fellow pilgrim. Somehow, we were intimidating, because most of the pilgrims who joined us on the other side of the Pyrenees were just starting out, and we had a kind of skedaddling inertia hurtling us forward. Our feet were in good working order: wounded, then toughened by a month of France, while these newbie pilgrims spent the first hour after stopping treating weeping blisters and wrapping ankles and knees in all sorts of bandages. There was some crying; there were some who were doing this international walking thing for the first time – retired people, overweight people, girls from the city, boys stunned to find nobody spoke French beyond the mountains we just crossed. The man running the *refugio* had mixed up a "*sopa de peregrino*", pilgrim soup, a big bin full of water, vinegar, and salt. People took turns soaking their feet in it. It's only pilgrim soup after four or five walkers have used the same batch.

I struck up a conversation with four German students washing their clothes in the back yard of the *refugio*, and the t-shirts they hung on the lines had strong lefty sentiments silk-screened into them, most of them quite anti-American. I hadn't made anything like the friendships I made when Petra and Jean-Philippe and I walked last time, but I was not really heartbroken about that. I felt as if I were preserving and honoring that journey by remaining apart. They all seemed like kids, and I was too old to be playing with them.

Nevertheless, I tried to tell them about the heritage I knew from the pilgrim road. Earlier in the day I showed them the famous poisoned river that Basques led unwary travelers to during the rowdy middle ages, so that there horses would drink and die and they could skin the beasts and eat their meat. None of the students were impressed. Nobody likes a know-it-all.

And the jokes I retold from the first pilgrimage didn't work any more. For example, there is a way that nearly every town in Spain is laid out, with the municipal sports arena (pool, gym, soccer field) to be placed at the outskirts and called the "*Polideportivo*". For those who have walked all day long, it's the first thing you see when coming into town, and imagining any sort of running, swimming, or jumping (and when you do imagine, it is always imagined done with a heavy backpack) casts the soul into a Cimmerian pit of despair. Petra, who had done the pilgrimage twice first, was the one who used to moan whenever she spied the latest *Polideportivo*, and we would have a rejuvenating laugh thinking of all that pole vaulting and gymnastics with a backpack still strapped to us.

But here, now, when I tried to crack a joke about the first *Polideportivo* I passed with the lefty German students, they failed to see the humor of the situation. Nobody was impressed. Nobody likes the guy who tells the same jokes over and over.

Jean-Philippe was miserable too, but for his own reasons. "It's so dangerous to return to a place like this," I told him.

"This food is terrible," he muttered.

"At least I don't have to eat any more damn omelets," I hissed. And that was what kept me going the second time: I felt much more at home in Spain, not just because I knew the language but also because of a familiarity with fried food, the love of conversation, and a desire to be just a bit self-destructive with pleasure (Spain is about twenty percent more dangerous than anywhere else: twenty percent more alcohol served in every drink, twenty percent more exposed wiring hanging from every wall, twenty percent more black tobacco in every filterless cigarette, twenty percent less seat belts on thrill rides and cars [same thing], twenty percent more children clad in flammable costumes next to festival bonfires flaring out of control; Spain is walking on one side of a high fence and hearing somebody on the other side rev up a buzz-saw or car or other big machine and somebody near them shouting, "Oye! Oye!"; God bless you, Spain.). And an odd comfort with this specific stripe of macho wasn't foreign to me, something they exported successfully to the New World centuries before.

We passed into La Rioja from Navarra and the landscape changed from sticky mud to purple hills with matching clouds; thistle, mowed hay, dill, the sweet anis Pacharán, brusque, obvious barmen, sandstone brown churches, smiling mild statues of the Virgin, the smell of frying potatoes, television in the dining room. I'd heard this joke before; I'd already dated this guy, this guy, this joke called the Camino; we had gone our separate ways six years before, and here I was, trying to have what is indelicately referred to as a "re-rack".

When one is working on something of any size, whether it is a book, a journey, or a child, one has the curse of time to fully realize that sometimes that thing will be a failure. A cheap imitation of the true thing, the original thing. And you have to go on, anyway. We call this feeling of finishing something that will fail, "exhaustion".

You get to see it all when walking: the graffiti on walls, for instance. In pre-dawn León, I came across some that was meant to bait skinheads: *Yo soy un Yanki Rojo Maricón Judeo Negro*. "I am an American Communist Gay Jewish Negro," with all the glib nasty words used, so if I were a better translator, I would offer: "I am a Yankee Commie Faggot Jew Nigger." In Europe, a "Yankee" is as marginal as a faggot or a commie. Graffiti is a part of the whole exhaustion of cities you witness when walking all the way – the exhaustions of cities at their outskirts, the sputtering, the self-unraveling, the petering out. There are death rattles: a half-finished factory, a promissory pile of cinderblocks, then freeway or dirt road, then trail again. Bruno Schulz's "Street of Crocodiles" is described like that: "The misfortune of that area is that nothing ever succeeds there, nothing can ever reach a definite conclusion. We shall always regret that, at a given moment, we had left the slightly dubious tailor's shop. We shall never be able to find it again. We shall wander from shop sign to shop sign and make a thousand mistakes."

More graffiti entering Villafranca del Bierzo: "*El rey es subnormal, y todo el mundo lo conoces*!": "The king is mentally retarded, and the whole world knows it!" Well, I hadn't been informed, as yet.

I knew every place along the road, and it was not as I knew it. One can be lost and found at the same time. There were ghosts at every turn: *there*, I said to myself in Viana, I had lunch in front of the church with an annoying Dutch man, Petra, and Matthias. And *there*, the crazy old lady Felisa, who had passing pilgrims sign in her book and offered "Figs, water, and love". A foot journey, whether to a pilgrim site or anywhere, is a love affair, I suppose; I'd had my chance with this lover. I wish I could travel with Anthony again; he is the best traveler I know.

I went to a bar far from the *refugio*, to be alone. There were six hard-drinking Madrileños who asked me to pull up a chair with them: they were impressed with my Spanish, and I'm easily flattered, although I quickly volunteered that I didn't quite understand the subjunctive. How is it going? they asked, and I told them what I was doing and my dilemma. It had been hard to come through again, a second pilgrimage. One of the men of the group took a moment from his avuncular, alcoholic happiness to say with great seriousness, "*Segundas partes nunca fueron buenas*," Second times never have gone well. Or Einstein said it another way: the definition of insanity is doing the same thing over and over and expecting different results.

# 2.

WE APPROACHED THE MONASTERY PARTAGE in Thiviers at the end of a long day of lupines, rich-red poppies, signs for approaching accordion festivals, shirts with horizontal stripes, butterfly trees in royal purple, the smell of pipe tobacco, force-fed ducks, lace in the windows.

As we entered the gate into the stone wall of the mon-astery, it was clear that it had fallen on hard times. A grand edifice with stained glass in every window, it was protected by tall boxwood hedges that had not been tended in a long time. Jean-Philippe looked at me. "Are you ready for another crrrreh-zee experience?" I am always perhaps too ready for a crazy experience, as long as it is always a new crazy expe-rience.

We walked in, and presented ourselves as St. Jacques pil-grims to a painfully skinny man not dressed in any habit I could recognize, and though he was pleased to have visitors, it was clear that the legal proceedings forbidding the Thiviers monks from haircutting, or exorcising, or practicing medicine may have been completed, but whatever energy it had had, renegade or religious, had been sucked from the group. In all, there seemed to be only four or five monks remaining, along with a little Algerian boy who looked to one of the men as his father. They seemed either silent or dispirited, and perhaps a little dicey. We were taken to the head of the order, a man who didn't look religious at all, who had a gut I'd call beer- before I'd call jolly-. He smoked, down to a nubbin, foul-smelling sto-gies (evidenced by five or six button-ends in his ashtray, from which he never strayed far) and had long smears of ash down a shirt he'd clearly worn for quite a few days. As a sweaty, dusty pilgrim, I felt cleaner. I certainly hoped he was wash-ing his hands before performing any unlicensed medicine. Or exorcisms, for that matter. Or haircuts.

But he was also welcoming, hadn't seen a pilgrim in months, and explained that he had always wanted to go to Santiago but something always held him back and that his monastery was free of charge and we will have your pilgrim passports stamped and dinner was at nine o'clock and would the skinny monk please take us to our rooms?

Rooms! For the entire time before and after Partage, Jean-Philippe and I had to share a room, step over one anoth-er's wet laundry, shut our ears to our idiosyncratic brands of snoring. We followed the monk down the hall. He had so many pimples. On the walls of the long cloister, there were prints of famous works of art, Van Gogh's mad sunflowers, Rembrandt's self-portrait, *The Birth of Venus*, *The Wreck of the Hesperus*. I passed a room that was the infirmary – dozens of beds, impeccably made, crisp cotton sheets, real hospital quality. Is this where the medicine was practiced without a license? Where was the Vietnamese fellow? Where was the machine that would take my Visa imprint?

My room was gigantic, big enough for five pilgrims, and I had my own bathroom, and my own pointless armoire. I opened up the big cumbersome thing, as I would naturally open up any pointless armoire, and found, stacked neatly, dozens of well-framed religious prints – the Virgin Mary as seen in the vision at Guadalupe, the Sacred Heart of Jesus, a rather nice Ascension, and so on. I thought of Van Gogh's *Sunflowers* in the hallway, and looked around my room. Not even a crucifix over the bed. But there was a long, delicious shower waiting for me.

While I hung up my hiking clothes to dry in the little garden of the cloister, one of the monks, rather upright but smiling, came by with an Algerian boy at his side. They were reading about Robin Hood. "Ah, you are English," he said after hearing me jerk out two or three words of French.

I corrected him: American – Yankee – a correction I have come slower and slower to make in these recent years under the recent administration.

He was unfazed. "Then you know this story of Robin Hood," said the monk, in order for the boy to see that I was not too strange a thing. "Perhaps you can remind us, who it was, who ruled in Nottingham that forced Robin Hood to steal from the rich? And over whom Robin Hood prevails?"

"I think it was the sheriff," I said.

The priest smiled, for I had given the right answer. "Ah yes, the *sheriff*." The boy recognized the word too, even in my pronunciation. He giggled. And the monk bade me come to dinner, and walked away, bathing in my answer.

Dinner was more than an hour away, so we went to a bar across the street. Jean-Philippe ordered us both a Pernod, though the name of the bar was "Bar Ricard", and Pernod is the competing anis. It was a locals bar, and everybody seemed to sport a mid-80s brush cut; they rolled up their sleeves. I spied a couple of disturbing pro Le Pen posters, but chose to concentrate on translating the handwritten signs, "*Pas de Credits*" (No Credit) and "*Reservee pour 3 viognos*" ("Reserved for the three winos"). The best part of the place was a little stumpy-legged dog that played with billiard balls for toys and had been trained to take your payment in euro bills behind the counter – "but he won't bring you change," Jean-Philippe pointed out. A lady came in and put her wallet on the floor and the dog opened it up and pulled the correct denomination out, a fiver. Monsieur Ricard, behind the bar, told us all, "Now he just takes a five. When he goes out on the town, he usually takes a twenty."

We were going to have a conversation, until we made the mistake of telling Ricard that we were staying in Thiviers. He did not ask us if we wanted another round.

But we were suitably lubricated, so we returned to the monastery and sat down to a long table in the refectory. They served us generous portions from a potato pie, a delicious chicken and peas and cheese and an untimely "Three Kings" cake, and in the slice I received I found buried in the crumbs a tiny ceramic Lisa Simpson figurine – and being the winner, I nearly chipped a tooth on the surprise.

The founder of our feast, still sloppy and smoky, started asking us all sorts of questions. They must have been so eager for company. "From Switzerland!" he said to Jean-Philippe. "Are you familiar with the work of your compatriot, Bakunin?" Bakunin ... Bakunin ... this name rang a bell. I looked over at Jean-Philippe, who had suddenly understood just a moment before me: Bakunin: the Swiss incendiary.

"Yes, he was from the town next to mine," said Jean-Philippe with a smile. I figured it all out about five seconds after him: we were being hosted by far-left communists.

Communist monks!

Oh, the way we all live in uncomfortable contradiction to ourselves. Conservative renegades, good thieves, fascinating bores, communist monks, Catholic homosexuals. This is also what makes us feel alone: we are one-of-a-kind monsters, neither fish nor foul. I thought of how ridiculous the monks of Thiviers seemed. I thought how ridiculous I was – how we all kept heading toward the end of our project, one we all knew would be a failure, surrounded by comfortable people who never have to live in contradiction. The communist monks of Thiviers live to this day, as far as I know, in a monastery deep in the heart of ultraconservative xenophobic Le Pen-following southern France. They have been abandoned by their own Church, reduced to a handful of bedraggled monks, and a boy, probably still considered armed and dangerous. For God's sake, they took down the religious iconography and replaced them with Van Goghs! And here we were, trapped with them!

And five seconds after this, the monk watching over the boy with the Robin Hood book asked me, "Tell me, do you have radical syndicalists in your country?" We were Yankee Commie Faggot Jew Niggers, the lot of us. We were all outsiders at this table, and could it be that this was the closest thing to "home" I have ever had on any of my journeys outward? Being who I am, there are moments, just now and then, when I have felt at home like this. But it only lasts for a night or so. Then home, or I, or both of us, skedaddles.

For the rest of the evening, we talked warmly of Bakunin and Woody Guthrie and the rise and fall of the Soviet Union, of causes not abandoned long after they were pointless or clearly a failure, and then of aporia, the losing of the way, and going on anyway. The monks of the Monastery Partage did not have a statue of Ste. Matthilde in the foyer, and they would not take our donation in the morning. "Just send us a postcard when you have reached your destination," said the stogie-smoking head of the order. I haven't sent them a card yet.

I wonder about myself sometimes: must everything be so flinty, so difficult? I am the one who reads the guidebooks only after I have made the journey, to discover that the sarcophagus I stood before was a great queen, or the ground I walked on was bloodied by Roland and his men. Only after. I read the guidebooks for nostalgia, but find instead that I have missed a thing I should have seen. "What is a divine mind," asks Jorge Luis Borges in a mere footnote to his essay "The Mirror of Enigmas". "I prefer an example. The steps a man takes from the day of his birth until that of his death trace in time an inconceivable figure. The Divine Mind intuitively grasps that form immediately, as men do a triangle. This figure (perhaps) has its given function in the economy of the universe."

What is nostalgia but this picking through the ruins of living – not living, but *remembering* living? Walking among the renegades in France was the adventure, and after entering comfortable, stomped-over Spain, it was as if I had entered the gift shop and never left it for a month, selecting souvenirs, when I had plenty of that back home.

And do you know what the real trouble is? I haven't changed my song one bit: I would still hang my head out that window in Tuscany and tell Anthony, ex or not, that I want to come back to this place. I always want to go back, even though I did go back once, and know for a fact it is never a smart idea. I returned to the pilgrim's route to Santiago a second time in order to walk a new stretch of it, and because I wanted to meet new walkers on that way. "*Segundas partes nunca fueron buenas*," Spaniards told me all the way to the end: "Second times never go well." And that's the truth I have to learn over and over and over. Think of Orpheus going after Eurydice, or Lot's wife's botched rescue from Sodom and Gomorrah, or Stoker's Dracula climbing out of the coffin in order to find his love again – second times never go well, Count. Nostalgia scares me, for it seems to turn gladness into ghosts, grief into grievance; one alone becomes only lonely.

# FAUX AMIS

## Apéritif

THAT NIGHT, I PREFERRED standing around out in the
farmyard in spite of the heat and manure. The sky was
cloudless, except in the far west where some cirrus clouds
might have been skywriting, formerly, blown askew, all the
signs, like these, rendered inscrutable. This was southwest
France: I'd always wanted to wallow in it. By now, however,
Jean-Philippe had shown me enough, and I wanted to get out,
go to Spain.

Pierrette, the new mistress of the house, had washed our
hiking clothes in some kind of deluxe machine that cycled
through an alarmingly two full hours, and I had been afraid
they would never dry in time for us to continue our walking
the next morning. But the stones of the old rugged sprawling
farmhouse that Michel called "Chateau La Rigalle" still held
the heat of the day, and, when I grasped my t-shirt on the line,
I thought that at least I had one less thing to fret about.

Jean-Philippe stepped out and spoke to me in an inhale,
two whole sentences, only possible in his language, "There
you are! I have come to tell you a little secret."

This pleased me; in the past few days, he'd been distant,
I thought, as if he'd had enough of me. "Oh?"

"Yes, it is about my uncle, Michel. Pierrette has told me

that his health is quite bad, and he is limited to the number of glasses of wine he may have, and also, he may have no dessert."

What did this have to do with me? How would this secret make the two of them closer? He adored his Uncle Michel. "*J'adore*," he'd said, (and I thought he was gushing a bit too much – adore!) and would never do anything to hurt him. But from the looks of Michel, he'd done enough to hurt himself, enjoyed the farm's fatted ducks, forbidden Armagnac, and unlicensed tobacco all too much. Jean-Philippe said, "So we must not make any yum-yum sounds when we enjoy the dessert my new aunt has made us."

This, I could do. I thought Jean-Philippe might forbid me the wine, which I needed more and more at these nightly *chambres d'hôte* pitstops, where Jean-Philippe spent the night jabbering away with the hosts while I sat trying to figure out how to eat tiny birds and complicated shellfish – or worse, finished my food long before anybody else had and stared at my empty plate while the rest ate like human beings.

"Oh-oh," said Jean-Philippe before walking back into the house. "Here is Coco. Don't get Coco excited." Coco was an emotionally damaged German Shepherd-Great Pyrenees mix, and in the three short hours since we'd arrived at La Rigalle, Coco had made it clear she did not like me.

Get her excited? Why was this screwed-up dog my fault? Dogs usually like me. Women usually like me. Men usually like me. Here, Jean-Philippe seemed to be avoiding me. Pierrette the hostess was terrified of me. And Michel did not seem to like me – why had he left his *chien bizarre* unattended?

Coco came near me and barked without making me feel specially singled out for hatred. It felt like a household hatred. But Michel and Pierrette Daccord (Daccord! The name smacked of welcome!) ran a *chambres d'hôte* and Jean-Philippe and I were sleeping in a big ancient room with big ancient (and separate) beds that had for mattresses layers and layers of cotton batting, which shifted like a regular bed but then did not shift back: initially comfortable until you rolled around (for sex, for instance, but that was only theoretical) and it didn't spring back into shape.

I found the bed a problem because I had been restless. Early on in our 25-kilometer hikes, I'd drop quickly into a sleep of recovery, but by now I'd grown stronger, and I would toss and turn, so that in the last four places where we'd stayed, I'd wake up and find Jean-Philippe had removed himself from the room to sleep well, and still, alone. The tossing and turning I blamed on being in a strange place, overstimulated and overtired. Did Jean-Philippe seem to be chilling toward me because he knew that my thoughts of France continued to smolder at the corner of my consciousness like an unattended tire fire at the dump? Or was I snoring?

Nobody was looking, so I kicked Coco away. She yipped and fled into the direction of sunset. The sun stayed up later here. It was nearly nine o'clock. During the day, when we were walking the Vézelay road on our way to the pilgrim city of Santiago in Spain, I made myself think of songs I knew and the names of plants and animals I recognized and, okay, God. At night, I wrote long passages in my journal about How to Handle the French, which I wasn't doing, not at all.

All of the men in France were not my type, either: skinny, emaciated, even, no power in their hands, all in their mouthy mouth, with all those puissant frontal labials. And their names! Yves! Jean! Michel! What kind of name is "Marie" for a man?

The heretofore timid Pierrette came out and poured me more of the Ricard, and dropped a second ice cube in. I stared at the caramel-colored cloud. Pierrette stared with me. Michel had taken Pierrette as his second wife less than six months ago, and I had figured she must be nearly half Michel's age; she could have been my wife in a very other life.

"*Un peu plus compose, Brian?*" She ran her hand through my freshly washed hair. Where had she gathered such boldness all of a sudden? Drink? I did feel a little more composed after a shower. I loved the feel of the bumpy bathmat on my sore feet after our long walks. Pierrette was trying so hard to make sure Jean-Philippe liked her. Pierrette didn't want her new nephew to think she was a gold-digger, I guessed, and so there was a lot of that business of kissing each other's cheeks, and Jean-Philippe didn't care, never discussed it with me. I tried not to create dramas where there weren't any, but it was difficult when I didn't speak the language – or rather, knew enough of the language to get myself into trouble.

"*Oui*," I tried, "*Je suis peu plus composé.*" I felt a sense of accomplishment when she nodded.

Jean-Philippe stepped up behind Pierrette. "Dinner is almost ready, Brian," he said. Was I crazy to think that there was a real cooling, that I was nothing more to him now that he was close to his family? He had introduced me as "*mon ami*", which sounded like lover to me.

"I have a favorite restaurant here in Pamplona," he had said the first time we'd met nearly six years ago, "and nobody to enjoy it with." I appreciated Jean-Philippe's stocky good looks (he was Swiss French, not skinny French), but took the invite as one pilgrim asking another, no more. We were on our first journey to Santiago, and he'd walked from his home, and that impressed me. I did let myself, even in scruffy, smelly state, enjoy his strong neck, absurdly tiny ears, gleaming black eyes.

The Pamplona restaurant turned out to be run by a chef from his small town near Bern, and he gave the two of us a table near the kitchen. I was complaining about a French colleague back home, with whom I'd been quarreling about cigarettes (she was pro, I contra), American temperament (I pro, she contra), and uncooked spinach (I pro, she horrified). We were in the same department, and had to work together. "If a person demands that you avoid them because they are at an impasse, what would you do?" I quizzed Jean-Philippe – extracting free advice on How to Handle the French. His English was perfect, from a year as a student abroad. He had picked up and retained a Cleveland accent.

He said, "The word 'demand' means something different

*en français*," rather than answering my question. "They are *faux amis*, false friends, *demander* and demand. *Demander* means simply to ask. Impasse is a *cul-de-sac* to us. If somebody demands something and there is an impasse, I would get back into my car and back out, go somewhere else. The person would be disappointed, but life will go on."

We shared a *salade* Landais, with duck *confit*, tomatoes, lardons; the wine was simple and cool, the cheese afterward strong. We tried to speak of pilgrims and maps, but we shared and discussed a love of woodworking, strong beer, and, most amazing of all, these long hiking trips that lasted weeks and months. At this point, I said, "Michael, my partner, doesn't like to go outdoors much like that. None of my boyfriends have liked to strap on a backpack."

Jean-Philippe had smiled, batted his eyes as if something merely small had been caught in them, rather than the sand and smoke I'd blown. "Send them to me," he said, a little deviously, "I'll train them."

And, disarmed, we continued to enjoy the meal, and as it progressed, I got the feeling we were ships passing in the night, or some cliché like that, and I let my heart be another cliché, and throb. In the end, I admitted my weakness to him: "Resolving things with my French colleague may be beyond my expertise," I said. "It could cost me my job."

"What you need is a proper translator," he said. "Somebody who knows the nuances of words, the *bon mots*." He gave me his address. When I returned to the States, he did save me, and my reputation. We continued to have phone conversations to the bitter end, and when it was over, I wished I'd had some excuse to call Jean-Philippe, beyond the usual Christmas cards.

A year after that, Jean-Philippe called me: would I like to do the pilgrimage again, this time from Vézelay, in central France? "Before I say yes," I said, "My French is *merde*." He laughed, but we were excited.

Now, Jean-Philippe said, as we went into the chateau for the dining room, "Pierrette has made a simple meal, but make sure you do not look like you are enjoying it."

## Amuse Bouche

Michel was already on his throne, paring his nails with a Laguiole knife. He was nearly eighty, his hands massive and once roughed up like quarried marble; now even that quality had been smoothed from the wearing down of age. The nails he cut at seemed made of goat horn, like the clasp of his knife. Besides the knife, before him he had his own special plate, and a tarnished silver napkin ring that held a dirty handkerchief. Often, when he talked, bits of spittle would form in the corners of his mouth, and he would have to wipe it off.

He was built like a king, or a big butane tank. His head was fleshy but small, and yet his knuckles were as knobby as the knees of a newborn colt. He made me examine my own hands there under the table, hands that always fascinate people because they are smooth, the palms of a blueblood. Here in France, with my walking stick, I had managed to build up the first calluses I'd had in years, and even a small, curious, painless blister at the tip of my index finger.

Michel had already given up trying to talk to me. What few words I could say in French made no sense to Michel, and because I made no sense, Michel apparently decided that he himself made no sense to me, either. "*Un Américain*," he said, and blew out his horsey lips.

In truth, mostly I didn't understand. Sitting night after night with other guests in these inns was like getting clues to a mystery. One person would say, "*Moo moo moo moo* cheese *moo moo* at the market *moo moo moo moo* strong *moo moo* bad (evil?) *moo* down there." And another would respond, "*Moo moo moo* Roquefort *moo* cloud." Now, entering the dining room, I heard Michel say to Jean-Philippe,

"*Moo moo Américain* Type," Type pronounced "teep", as he tossed back a whole glass of something gold in his own private unmarked bottle. When he lifted his hand, I noticed that half of the man's pinky was missing.

Jean-Philippe said, "*Moo moo moo moo*?"

Michel answered, "*Moo Américain* Teep!: My country, my family, my religion. Is it true for this *Américain* too, *moo*?"

Jean-Philippe turned to me. "Is it true?"

Pierrette burst from the kitchen with a plateful of *tartines de foie gras*: thin, toasted bread with powerful, simple diabolical medallions of rich meat. "I am sorry," she sang in the upper register so much of French needed to be spoken in, and "*Moo moo moo*", which I figured meant, "for keeping you waiting," but may as well have been, "But I had to slaughter the ducks myself and extract their livers."

She placed a *tartine* in front of me first, tiny but potent, an amusement for the mouth, foreplay, and I waited as she gave one to Jean-Philippe, and finally one to herself. On Michel's plate, she set a crusty baguette for him to slice. No treat for Michel, but a task. I put my *tartine* completely into my mouth and experienced the thick salty star-matter of flavor, and almost forgot my promise to Jean-Philippe. As if she knew I was about to show some sign of pleasure, Pierrette reached my hand and gripped as her aged husband cut circles of bread, which he did in the way he might cut up an animal, a thing he'd done all his life. It seemed a crime to use such a fine knife for this trifling job. But bread could be a cruel business: I would trudge into towns at the ends of these walking days exhausted, footsore, and see the word "*pain*" over one of a dozen bakeries, and I'd think the word for bread was a secret torture for an English speaker.

Michel continued to talk to Jean-Philippe as if the other two of us were not in the room. Pierrette whispered to me, and I understood all the words, not a *moo* in the mix: "Don't you think my husband is a little crazy?" But she said "bizarre" and the word sounded more like an appellation for ghouls. I didn't know how to respond; I was a guest of both husband and wife. I would rather think about the *tartine*'s taste, the thick pasty quality meat could have. I wanted more. Now I was done and the first course seemed hours away, and I could not speak and I could not move my food around on my plate. Where were my elbows? Was that an itch? Should I drink all my wine?

Michel said, "Pierrette, the *moo* pottage, for God's sake."

# The Soup

Pierrette was up at once. When she opened the kitchen door, I could just see in. It was lit only by dusk, and a picturesque mess: cartons of eggs from the henhouse, too many tomatoes from the garden, a half-chopped onion, three melons, various limp and perked lettuces. It smelled like all of Gascony – like a used wet chamomile teabag. I'd noticed that the outdoor and indoor worlds of rural France sometimes switched places, ferociously ordered in nature (all those trimmed hedges!), gone back to the wild in the house. Chateau La Rigalle, a house built for some sprawling extended family and its servants, was now occupied by an aging farmer and his eager young wife and the occasional agritourist. Pierrette, obviously, had done her best to keep up a number of the rooms (I'd snooped around earlier) but simply given up on others. Under the stairway, a complete chaos of dusty garden implements, buckets, and various leather and rusted metal implements for inexplicable tasks. The dog, too, was feral, didn't even respond to civilized bribery.

On the Chemin de St-Jacques, the road to Santiago, however, I'd seen just the opposite. I was walking just that morning through a forest of perfectly aligned trees that had been planted under Napoleon. The weeds and wildflowers looked like houseplants released back into the wild with their spotted fronds and symmetrical leaf arrangements; the cows looked mascaraed and coiffed. Now and then, deer would spring out on the trail and walk right by, fatted and tame. It made me say, "Let's have an expensive meal in town tonight."

Jean-Philippe apologized. "We have to eat with my uncle tonight; he will make us an expensive meal, but it will be free."

"Then how can I pay you for all the help you gave me with my colleague last summer? I have to do something to show my appreciation."

He laughed. "Do you remember what I said when you first asked what my fee was for the dealings of that negotiation?"

He had said it was free: "*C'est libre.*" I told him so.

He laughed again. "*'C'est libre'* doesn't mean it is free, actually. It means that you are free to give what you can give."

I felt a hole in my stomach open, then shrink too rapidly. He laughed and laughed and laughed, so I must have been blushing. "*Pas de problème*," he said, and pushed me off balance with my top-heavy backpack. I fell on my back like a turtle. Overhead, two swallows cavorted, as merry and reckless and harmless as blunted art scissors. He was laughing even harder, and from this angle, despite so many weeks spent together, I noticed for the first time that a light shone through a place in his nostrils – he'd had it pierced at some point. For the rest of the afternoon, I insisted that I write Jean-Philippe a check, give him a generous fee, but he wouldn't listen.

Pierrette bounded through now with a baroque tureen full of *pottage de*-what? It was orange. I'm not a picky eater, but orange food sometimes spooks me.

She ladled soup into our shallow bistro bowls and she gave me my portion first again, so that I had to sit, fidgeting, while everybody else waited in silence. "*Bon*, Brian," Michel must have realized that he had only been talking to his nephew the entire meal and made an awful effort to engage me. I wished he had not. The only thing worse than not being talked to is being talked to. "*Moo moo* where in the United States do you live and *moo*?"

"Chicago," I said. I was using my tight professional smile, and that made me mad, because I was on vacation, after all.

"Ah," said Michel expansively, and then, as Pierrette spooned for him not pottage but a thin broth from a special gilded bowl (a handful of sliced carrots floated in it, a mockery of hearty fare), he said, "*Moo*, Chicago, Illinois." I nodded. "But you know," Michel leaned closer, "we call it here in France, Illy-NWAH, *moo*."

Before I could unscramble and feel offended by this, Coco bounded in, and sat at her master's chair. Michel gave her bread. She loved the bread. If only this dog would stop hating me. Then she'd get something good to eat.

The pottage steamed but it did not burn my mouth. This seemed a miracle, because soup, like donut shop coffee, usually seared and scalded rather than tasted. When soup could be tasted, it was mostly salt. But this was herbal, even though it was made of carrots and squash. Somehow they were root vegetables without the rooty taste – she must have used tiny sweet carrots and acorn squash no larger than acorns. It was a candy version of soup, the texture of oiled silk, I thought, and distracted thus, I realized that, in my bowl, it was gone.

I ran my spoon frantically along the bottom, and what that did was make me aware that I was probably being rude. Did people scrape their plate in France? Did they sop with bread? Michel was still yammering about what he did and did not know about Chicago.

"Tell your uncle that Illinois is actually the bad pronunciation of the name the Native Americans of my region called the land. It would be like me calling him Franchise."

Jean-Philippe was silent for a moment, sipped his soup, then said, "*Comment*? I mean, what?"

This was the other problem with the language gap – I had only baby talk to convey complex ideas. If they were *moo*ing, I was *goo*ing. I really wanted to get up and go to the bathroom, but I could just do that once, realistically, during a meal, already dallying with the rude, without seeming ill. But the air was thick at that moment and soup, dammit, was gone.

"*Excusez-moi*," I hit upon it – "But I must wash my hands because Coco licked them." Both Michel and Jean-Philippe looked at me doubtfully. Coco growled when I stood, that bitch.

Still, I fled. The bathroom was in an unlikely place, built off the kitchen. I closed the door to the bathroom. It had been all girlied up by Pierrette with certain odd concessions to her tough old farmer husband. A tiny cigar box made of Lalique glass and framed pictures of hunters matted with exposed cardboard corrugation. And potpourri, even it was woodsy potpourri. The bathroom was old and damp and windowless. Pierrette probably had to scrub it each day to keep it from going back to the wild.

I looked at my face in the mirror, then held my hands up to it, as if I couldn't see properly unless mediated by reflection. I'd read in some men's health magazine that one should sing Happy Birthday to oneself two complete times while washing one's hands. I turned off the water reluctantly after the third refrain, and dried my hands. In the hallway, I ran into Pierrette. She pressed me against the hallway wall with an imploring look I had no time to register. "Brian," she said, "you must help me, I can not be around that man another day." What was strange: she said it in an almost unaccented English.

Before I could respond, we heard Michel shout, "Pierrette! *Salade!*"

## The Salad

Pierrette stopped her intense pressure and slipped into her kitchen. I realized she'd been clutching my shirt at an awkward place where a button was, and I had to tuck myself in again. This felt like a racy thing to do. I stepped back into the dining room. Jean-Philippe hardly acknowledged my return, for he was in deep, serious conversation with his uncle about – me? He was saying, "*Moo moo* depart from him/it *moo moo moo* early in the morning *moo moo* when we are not seeing each other." What? What? Had I heard correctly? Was he plotting secretly to ditch me along the trail soon? And was this how I was to find out? He says it right in front of my face?

"*Ah, quelle déception!*" Michel laughed ruefully.

"Deception?" I blurted.

"Brian!" Jean-Philippe seemed surprised I'd slipped back to the table without his noticing. "Is it your birthday? Have we missed the celebration of your birthday?"

"No, why?"

"We can hear you singing happy birthday to yourself in the bathroom!" He repeated this to Michel in French, and they laughed together. But I wondered, if they had heard me sing happy birthday, had they not also heard Pierrette moan about her husband?

Pierrette bounded in with a smile and a great platter of greens, arugulas and radicchios and butter lettuces that adorned chunks of the most perfect tomatoes I had ever seen. Pierrette offered the plate to me first, with a look that, to her step-nephew and husband might pass for friendship to a stranger, but appeared to me as desperate entreaty. And also: if I got the plate first, I would have to wait again as the others filled their plates, and then they would wait expectantly while I fumbled with my inelegant American hands (Jean-Philippe had taught me just a week ago how to hold a knife and fork in proper European manner and I had felt like a child, *goo*) and I thought, all right, all right, don't rush me, and I spooned a half dozen chunks of lightly dressed tomatoes onto my plate.

Jean-Philippe was swift and thoughtless. Michel stabbed one at a time, and I realized he too was a child in Pierrette's dining room, and was controlled like one. It came to me that she was torturing her new husband. "That's enough," she said in French. "You know what the doctor said about *moo*." Michel immediately obeyed, and put one slice of tomato back. I stabbed one of my own, not thinking about its taste but forced, suddenly, to do so once it entered my mouth. It reminded me that scientists call it a fruit, not a vegetable. It was also some kind of animal, the firm fleshy chambers held the guts and seed that burst in my mouth, and I had the feeling I was a caveman, one that had killed and sunk its teeth into a still-warm beast, and my hands clenched my knife and fork and my head pitched back and the flavor ran down my throat like blood. Jean-Philippe's eyes widened; it was just a tomato, he said with his eyes, don't upset Michel.

To hide my pleasure, I put another tomato in my mouth. But I was eating too quickly. When playing the role of the lost penny, I'd learned to spread my meals out in artificial ways to avoid sitting listlessly, awkwardly at the end of a course. I'd take a bite, count to five, swallow, count to five, stab again, one-two-three-four-five, BITE, one-two-three-four-five, CHEW, one-two – but this only heightened the pleasure, here, of the perfect tomatoes. Nevertheless – one-two-three-four-five, BITE, CHEW, one-two-three –

"Brian! I asked you if you wanted the last two tomatoes so that Pierrette can remove the plate." Swimming at the bottom of the bowl were two half-moon slices. I wanted them for their taste, for something to do while they talked of departures and deceptions.

But wait (one-two-three-four-five), why would he offer me the tomatoes? For my birthday? He knew they were delicious. And he was a businessman, never too timid to take what he wanted (one-two-three-four-five). Was this some sort of strategy? Was something even better coming to the table, some new magical course that would also have two bites left for somebody, two bites that would have to go to Jean-Philippe, or I would seem rude? *Quelle déception*!

As if in answer, Pierrette slipped quietly into the dining room with perfectly dressed lardons of duck, obviously a duck that had been waddling around in the yard earlier that day, slow-cooked in a deep stone oven. The aroma was golden, too. I stabbed the last two tomatoes anyway. Michel watched my boarding house reach, appalled.

"Delicious," I said, and immediately regretted it.

Pierrette flashed me a version of my tight business smile. Jean-Philippe did not.

## The Duck

Pierrette gave Michel the duck to carve. He took his knife

– was it the same knife he used for the bread? For killing ducks? For paring his horny nails? For scraping sheep shit off the soles his shoes? Michel carved the bird as if it needed carving, but the meat simply fell off the bones. Pierrette had taken even that master-of-the-house task away from Michel, for it was sufficiently cut. Michel put some on his nephew's plate. Then Pierrette gave him some more broth, and took the platter of duck to the center of the table. There were potatoes in their skins, too, and warm white asparagus.

Jean-Philippe looked up to his uncle just then with eyes narrowed by an indulgent smile, and once again I could see light coming from his nose, through it, from the eternally setting sun out the window. He was mostly in silhouette, and the pinpoint glint was striking. He was a man who'd had a nose ring, completely capable of rebellion, of acts cruel and anarchic – tattoo-getting, city-wall-tagging, middle-of-rural-France-ditching, and me left to be eaten by Coco the gorilla dog.

"Eat, eat," Michel suddenly shouted. It was supposed to be a fatherly hostly command, but it sounded resentful, and after I let it slip out that I'd been enjoying the tomato (that little easily translatable "delicious" had been like a floorboard's squeak during a nighttime jewel heist), Michel was watching me. The duck pieces were bite-sized. To cut it in two would be a fuss. I stabbed. I cut. I tasted. I forgot to hide my pleasure.

To replace any withering word he might have for me, Jean-Philippe let his fork clatter to the plate.

"Moo moo moo moo *seventy years* moo moo."

Jean-Philippe translated for the first time that evening, "My uncle says he has been eating ducks every day for his whole life, and he still enjoys them!" This seemed both possible and wistful, for Michel couldn't eat them any more, if Pierrette had anything to do with it. And I was having trouble enjoying the – yes – succulent quality of the duck because he had succumbed to flavor.

Pierrette caught Michel putting salt on his broth and she nearly screamed at him, "You know what the doctor told you!"

I looked over at Pierrette. She'd been seated for no more than two minutes, enough time to spoon a little of her own food onto a plate, when Michel *moo*'d another request, feeble retaliation. She fought for a moment, saying it was something he shouldn't have, but stopped in the middle of her protest, stood, and took the long way around the table, duck-duck-goose, tilting toward both Michel and me, for we shared the corner at the end.

When Pierrette leaned toward us, her eyes rolled on the incline like two marbles, aswim within with violet fins, thought only I could see this, and I wondered, was she signaling me to follow her, or telling me to regard the slave-driver that was her husband? Or was she simply rolling her eyes sarcastically at the ridiculous task/man/situation?

Jean-Philippe had remembered together, earlier that day, a night in Spain on our last pilgrimage, when we were having a laugh at our Iberian hosts. We'd looked for a vegetarian plate for Jean-Philippe and flummoxed the locals – what was vegetarianism?, they wanted to know – you eat a first course and then, what?, a second course? We only found on the menu a thousand things that came out of the sea, octopus the most recognizable. Jean-Philippe capitulated to the "vegetable salad", which was flaked with tuna.

And here in France, after he had expressed his dread of returning to the cuisine of Spain, I reminded him of the vegetable salad. "*Exito*!" I had said, to cheer him up.

He asked me, as we walked along, whether "*Exito*" was the Spanish word for "Let's Exit," because he was ready to make an *exito* any time now.

"*Exito* is Spanish for 'success'." Spanish, I knew, and I looked forward to a time when Jean-Philippe would depend upon me, for a change, and I would feel like, well, a man, not feckless, on the run.

But we'd been in Spain together before. Jean-Philippe had found his own solution, back then, to the problem of sitting alone at a Spanish table while I and the others *habla*'d on and on. Jean-Philippe told me after just such a dinner that sometimes he would listen to our conversations and take one or two of the words he knew or thought he knew and conjure the conversation: "My friend (my lover?) was an embarrassed bullfighter but he ended up in the pharmacy business until he broke his toe (finger?) and worked with prisoners (and himself?) for his goats in the trees." Jean-Philippe said of this, "It can be surreal, but it can also be accurate."

"That's the silliest thing I've ever heard," I'd said, even though we had talked about goats getting into the trees. "'*Embarazada'* is a false friend, too, and doesn't mean embarrassed. It means pregnant."

But here at the dinner table in Chateau La Rigalle, I'd run out of opportunities for counting to five, wearied of the mooing, and the duck was gone, so I tried Jean-Philippe's trick myself.

Jean-Philippe was saying, perhaps, "Pierrette, if she were a man, would be a master of the ducks."

Michel perhaps said, "Only a man can be master of the ducks."

"You must be careful," it seemed Jean-Philippe was saying, "or Pierrette will depart from you as well, what a deception!"

Michel laughed and reached for his nephew's glass of wine. He held it out to him, naughty, and said before he drank deep from it, "And where do you think she will go to make her omelettes?" Maybe that's what he said: omelettes.

Pierrette reentered and let clatter onto the table before Michel a platter of noodles smothered in a simple sauce – a béarnaise. Beside it, a bowl of wild rice, and smaller bowl with gray lentils. Food meant for the poor and Desert Fathers. The béarnaise looked great, though.

Michel looked pleased. He saw that I was eyeing the plate, too. He said, "Would you like some?"

Pierrette snapped, "No, I made *moo* for you." And then I thought she may have muttered, "I hope the béarnaise burns through your internal organs," in English. And that's when I began to wonder whether Pierrette might be poisoning her

husband, weakening him and blaming it on his delicate condition. I watched the old man eat directly from the bowls,
because they were his alone. It was as if he'd been starved.
He inhaled the food, paying no attention to texture or taste;
Pierrette may as well have set the bowls on the floor for Coco.
Before long, the energy drained out of Michel, and he was as
gray as his lentils. She must be killing him.

Michel began to talk with food in his mouth. Now it didn't
even sound like mooing to me. I often elect not to rent the
headphones for in-flight movies, but would sit and piece together the pantomime story, nonetheless. That was what it
was like to watch Michel now. The way Michel contorted his
lips and nose while he chewed made it impossible to know
whether he was complaining or praising, and whether the
dis/pleasure was for the food, Pierrette, his health, or the
*Américain* Teep next to him.

Jean-Philippe would not converse with me. He was too
busy eating, and probably couldn't understand his uncle
either. But Pierrette understood him, for he said something
mid-bite, and I was able to hear, loud and clear,

"No dessert for you!" Pierrette said it in French, and got
up to get the dessert.

Michel pulled his filthy handkerchief off his lap, wiped
the corner of his mouth, rolled the handkerchief up again,
and slid it into its silver ring with the nubbin pinky. He got up
and said something about closing the barn, before the *moos*
got out. Coco skittered out with him.

## The Dessert

At last, it was only Jean-Philippe and I together in the dining
room. But Jean-Philippe only half-smiled. He stabbed the last
two bits of duck on the platter, just as I suspected he'd do. If
only I could drink a little more wine. Life always required just
a little more fine tuning. To kill time, I looked at the bouquet
of wildflowers Pierrette offered the dining room table, com-

mon daisies, but of different colors, all messily stuffed into a tall vase. They wilted, leaned, hung. They were beautiful. What confection, I wondered, would Pierrette unveil for dessert?

I was about to say something to Jean-Philippe, something conspiratorial, but outside, I could hear Coco barking like a maniac, with one single-syllable admonition from Michel to quiet her: "*Moo!*"

"I'm going to carry some of these empty plates in for Pierrette," I said.

"She can handle it," Jean-Philippe warned, but I ignored him.

There were sauces all over the plates. In Spain, it would be impolite to lick plates or daub them with bread. Jean-Philippe hated Spain soon after learning that, on our last pilgrimage. I put the plates down on an empty counter while Pierrette, absorbed in dessert preparation, kept her back to me, perhaps not sure who was with her in her kitchen. I ran a finger across the béarnaise bowl – a life-risking gesture. The flavors of pickled capers, sharp parsley, and tarragon and lemon, all separately discernable but also married, made me stick my finger in again.

Pierrette said, without turning from her work, "I want to go to Paris tonight. I have a sister there. But I have no money and I have no credit cards. I would be able to pay you back when I get to Paris."

I stepped into the hall separating dining room from kitchen. "I don't know," I said, "I'm not sure."

"I just want you to take me to the train station, and drive the car back for Michel. Michel needs the car. That is all I'm asking." I wanted to go south, to leave France, to get into Spain. She was asking me to go in the opposite direction.

"Perhaps." One of my misgivings, one she could not know about, was my need for purity on this pilgrimage. I had not been in a car for over a month, and wanted to make sure that all the movement I ever made was on foot. I couldn't drive standard transmission, either. And still I said, "Perhaps."

"Go back to Jean-Philippe. Michel is returning from the barn. I will bring something sweet to you very soon."

It was, at first, a disappointment: ice cream. But then, it was not just ice cream, but homemade ice cream with nuts and a perfumed honey with orange blossom and rose and something else, what? – chestnuts, Jean-Philippe explained in a quick aside when I nudged him, like a child interrupting the grownups, honey made from chestnuts.

We were silent after that, listening to Michel outside, yelling at the ducks. I kept thinking of Jean-Philippe giving me the slip. He had the maps! He had the guidebooks! And they were all in French: the direction "*tout droit*" meant "all to the right", and I would have turned right at every intersection. But "*tout droit*" really meant "go straight." Lost, I thought, I'm lost.

"Will you help me with the coffee?" Pierrette asked in simple enough French. Now that I had carried in the plates, breaking the rules about men in the kitchen, I was being invited to smash away at etiquette. Jean-Philippe smiled warmly, to encourage me to follow Pierrette, because he did not want to seem insensitive to my forlorn presence, counting to five and spreading out the potty breaks and bolting my food. I hate pity, almost as much as I hate being misunderstood. But I knew what Pierrette wanted. I followed her into the kitchen once more.

She began as if she had never asked me to take her to Paris, nor grabbed me by the button and made me tuck in my pants. "Where have you been walking from?" she wanted to know, as she tapped little spoons against this carafe and that.

"Vézelay," I said, and that had been nearly four weeks ago, ancient history.

And Pierrette, being French, replaced honesty with brutality, or mistook the two, when she patted my belly and said, "But you're still fat!" Perhaps it wasn't such a brutal thing to say in French. In any case, she had done the thing: I would now need to prove myself to her, would need to show her that I was more than met the eye. What did she want? She wanted me to help her get away.

"Are you poisoning your husband?" I said, holding up the emptied plate with the drying béarnaise glaze. We could both be direct; time was short.

She laughed. "He is poisoning himself. I do not have to do anything."

"Didn't you know what you were getting yourself into before you married him?"

She pouted, let a tiny spoon patter out of her grip, as an example of powerlessness. "You are cruel," she said, "how can you know a person until you have been intimate with them? He was a prosperous farmer! His name is Daccord! I have always wanted to be the Madame of a *chambre d'hote*! I wanted to make his life happier." I looked out the window and deciphered a sign while she sang her lamenting aria: "The picking of mushrooms is strictly forbidden here."

"Where would you go to make your omelettes if you left Michel?"

"My omelettes?"

I could hear Michel coming in through the side door; the ducks were in their place. So were the sheep. "Pierrette, I want you to help me, if I am going to help you," I said.

"But you will help me? Then good!"

"I think Jean-Philippe wants to ditch me."

"Ditch? Throw you in a ditch? I have just washed all of your clothing."

"No, I think he's tired of me and wants to get away from me while I'm not watching."

"Oh," she said, picking up that little spoon again, then: "Oh! Yes, well. He has said something like this to us at the table, as well, I think." Then she picked up the coffee service and headed toward the dining room. I had nothing to carry, and I felt foolish following her, a servant to a servant.

Michel and Jean-Philippe had been talking quietly when we came in. They stopped abruptly. Jean-Philippe said to me, "Would you like more of the ice cream," as I sat down and began to fool around with my coffee, putting sugar and cream into it. I like my coffee black.

"No," I said, and thought I'd try a little French. When we'd gone to hotels that were full, they told us that they were "*complet*". I was full, too. I said, "*Je suis complet*." I smiled.

Pierrette began to giggle, then Jean-Philippe looked down into his coffee and sputtered into it. Michel did not laugh but made a face at the *Américain* Teep that spoke volumes: What An Idiot.

"What's so funny?" I appealed not to Jean-Philippe, but to Pierrette, under my breath, as if this were not a dinner for four but one for twenty, and only those closest might hear me ask.

Jean-Philippe answered, "You just said that you were pregnant."

Pierrette got up again and left the room, laughing like some cruel girl in an opera, given an entire laughing song to show off her coloratura. She only laughed once she was out of the room, however, as if being polite.


## The Cheeses

From far away, from a place perhaps beyond the kitchen – the barn, the forest itself, I heard a cart roll ever closer to the dining room. It was a dreadful sound, one I'd learned about in the past few weeks. It was the cheese course coming, after all these rich foods, and I would be expected to select from among the mushroomy camemberts and tangy roqueforts and chalky camemberts and nutty cantals. There'd be grapes, too, and probably a sugary bottle of sauterne, and then I would have to eat it all, even when I was paralyzed with so much food and isolation and drink and stimulation. I would moan and it would be mistaken for a sound of pleasure, and they'd serve me more, or, if Jean-Philippe mistook me for making another yum-yum sound tonight, he would, indeed, depart from me, what a deception!

The cart trundled closer. I could hear its rickety wheels

rumble along uneven slatted floors, drop silent as it passed over a hallway rug, clatter back to life on the floor, silently run again on another rug. It was like that little boy on his Big Wheel in *The Shining*.

"I must go to the bathroom," I said, interrupting whatever it was that Jean-Philippe was saying to Michel, and I skittered off. I met Pierrette at the door of the dining room and was blocked, trapped, by the cheese cart. Everything I had imagined would be on the cart was indeed there, and more – an armagnac and those melons I'd seen, sliced in quarter moons, baby-aspirin orange.

"Where are you going?" she hissed. Did Michel know she could speak English? Did Jean-Philippe?

I didn't answer, but ran on, locking myself in the bathroom. I sat on the toilet, not taking down my pants. I felt breathless and dogged. In a basket at my side was a booklet of crossword puzzles, most half-done and abandoned. I had such a basket in my bathroom. A familiar sight made strange – the worst thing that could happen. France would have been easier for me if there had been no samenesses, no cognates in the language, no comparable table manners, their favorite food a dog dish, their heads green, their feet blue, setting sail daily in a sieve. But no: *crossword puzzles*. And, if the answers were any indication, idiotically easy ones, with words like "noir", "fidélité", and "aussi".

Oh the French, I thought; but what bothered me most was that if I had been French, I would have been the most insufferable Frenchman of them all. I would have ruined myself long before Michel on pleasure.

Pierrette knocked on the door. She said in a low voice, "Tonight, you will meet me? I will take the Renault to Périgeux and board the train to Paris. If you come with me, I will show you all the sights of Paris. I cannot go alone!"

Beyond the door, beyond Pierrette, beyond the cheese cart, I heard Michel and Jean-Philippe burst into conspiratorial laughter. I was sure they were discussing my pregnancy again, or my birthday, or the developing plans to abandon me.

I'd had enough of Jean-Philippe! He drank beer at 10 in the morning! He brushed his teeth the way I hated! How could he do this to me? I opened the door only a crack, even though there was nothing indecent about me. I spoke through the wedge. "I'll leave my backpack in the hall," which was supposed to be some sort of assent, only indirect, only, I hoped, misunderstandable: Not "yes", not at all.

"Three o'clock. In the morning."

I sighed. She blew me a kiss as I closed the door. Was that to be expected as well, the kissing?"

# Digestif

After I washed my face in the old farm sink where the hot water boiled out of one spigot and the cold came out of the other, I found the dinner abruptly over; Jean-Philippe already retreated to his own bed. There'd be walking to do tomorrow, as usual.

The big windows were over Jean-Philippe's bed. To look through it, I stood over him and crossed my arms. If I looked menacing there, to him, then so what. It would have been the first time this trip. Outside, I could see, in the perpetual gloaming that seemed to be the lux aeterna of southern France, Michel shooing two ponies. As purple shadows, they looked overfed, balloon animals. I said so to Jean-Philippe. "It's as if he doesn't know that by feeding them too much, he's not caring for them, but harming them. They're not like his ducks, you know."

Jean-Philippe was quiet for a moment, and I thought he had fallen asleep already. Then he said, "He knows." It was funny, how I could not see Jean-Philippe in the dark of the room, but I could see Michel just fine, though he was grainy like a black and white photo made from blowing up a negative too much. He tapped his ponies with a stick. Jean-Philippe said, "He's old. He wants to be a farmer and run his *chambre d'hote* and live a life as he has always done, and he cannot do it, not without help. It's humiliating for him."

Just as Michel almost coaxed the horse in, Coco bounded out of the house, barking, spooking the beasts. Michel grabbed Coco roughly by the collar and dragged her into the house without saying anything, but knowing as anybody would know that Coco was a worse than useless animal. He had to go searching for the horses.

Jean-Philippe made little mousy movements in the dark below me, trying to make a comfortable place in the cotton batting for himself. In the dark, I could almost forget about his nose ring hole. I asked him, "Tonight, at dinner, you were talking about something with Michel, what was it?" Perhaps he would admit it. Perhaps I could get him to bring his disenchantment into the open, for once, and I could thwart his plans to bolt.

"About something?"

"About something that was '*quelle déception*'."

Jean-Philippe laughed with his mouth shut. "Oh yes. Last winter, when there seemed no hope that you and I might ever get together, I cheered myself up by going to Sri Lanka. On the first day there, somebody stole my camera. *Quelle déception*!"

I watched Michel plod back toward the house. I knew Michel could not see me, not in the dark, not with his bad eyesight. Nevertheless, I made a single sliding step away from the window. Michel suddenly stopped – aware of my movement? But no. He clutched his stomach, bent over for a minute, and coughed. It took Michel another minute before he could stand up. Tomorrow, I thought, he'd be doing all this completely without Pierrette's help.

I took a pleasure in feeling the little calluses at the bases of each finger from the walking stick, from wringing out my own clothes when washing them – except for tonight, when, as a helpless child, I let Pierrette wash them in her machine. Wait! I couldn't go to Périgeux in the car – my clothes were still on the line.

I stubbed my toe trying to find my own bed: the furniture here was ponderous, yet fussy, like Michel. Sitting on the edge of my uncomfortable bed, I wished Pierrette had offered me a nightcap of some kind, after all that sugar and caffeine; it would be hours before I'd be able to fall asleep. And she would be coming into the hall at three in the morning, beckoning to me with her damn perfect English, impossible to misunderstand.

"Jean-Philippe," I said in the dark, "we have to talk about something." He didn't answer right away, and I wondered if he'd fallen asleep.

# TRAVELS WITH CHARLEY

I N THE FALL OF 2001, IN A month that will live in infamy, I returned to Chicago after being away from it for sixteen years. I had been living in San Francisco. What was I – they wanted to know, there and here – out of my goddam mind?

But San Francisco is like the domed city in *Logan's Run*; when you turn 30, your hand crystal starts blinking red, and you have two choices: turn yourself in believing that you will be reborn during the flameout at Carousel, or run like hell, hoping Michael York is your hunka-hunka Sandman when it comes time to be shot down like a rabid dog. I am exaggerating, but there is something deeply transient about San Francisco, The City of Thirty-Year-Olds. People say things like, "The next town I live in will be Boston." For homos, it's certainly not Kansas any more, but people do come and go so quickly there.

When I returned to Chicago, my best friend and her family came to my flat to celebrate the ninth birthday of their daughter Miranda (Horoscope: Pony-Crazy on the cusp of "My little sisters can have my Barbies now no they can't yes they can no they can't"). Miranda walked dreamily through my flat, one decorated by a gay man who has sacked Europe of its bric-à-brac thirty times over. "Hand over your precious tchatchkies, or my checkbook gets it!" Breakable Delft gewgaws, sofa-sized but challenging art on the walls, rare books, baby hybrid veggies in the icebox. Miranda picked up a horseshoe I was using as a paperweight, and sighed. "I like Hank," she decided. "He's *fancy*." While they incinerate you in San Francisco if you're over 30, in Chicago, though you don't get to be gay any more, you can be *fancy* for the rest of your natural life.

I am not saying Chicago is without its quirks. In the nearly ten years since my return, I have learned that the phrase, "nearly legal" is a term used as a great compliment. "This parking place is nearly legal." or "What Mayor Daly did to Meigs Field with those bulldozers was nearly legal." But middle American idiosyncrasies and hypocrisies, I not only understand but in some ways perpetuate; I had grown up in Michigan, after all, and went to college in Chicago, and maintained my level-headed Midwestern-ness to flaky California, where showing up for the job was commendable by not ever losing that job.[1]

Back in Chicago, I was delighted – delighted! – to find fresh water aquariums in high-end restaurants with carp and pike patrolling where I expected to see clown and lion fish. Native grasslands in the park – weeds as flowers! And there was that Lincoln Square neighbor (a woman I annually assumed died each winter because I never saw her come or go from her house until late spring), having surrounded her bungalow with an English style garden full of long spiky flowers, mossy rockeries, and tomato plants and corn stalks lovingly trellised as ornamental plants, who installed a little bench just off the sidewalk and stabbed into the lawn a little jigsaw-cut and painted image of a fat lady gardener, bent over, the words, "Welcome to My Garden!" scrawled on her ass. Not a foot away from that message, on a decal in the bungalow window, was the sign, "We Call Police!" If there is any image emblematic of the Windy City Way, I would choose that. That, or the place in Andersonville where a parking meter was installed right next to a fire hydrant.[2]

When I saw the welcome/unwelcome signs, when I saw that the little pigs in Chicago built their houses of wolf-proof bricks rather than the feckless houses of sticks in San Francisco, when I bought my first hot dog at Al's Fun in the Bun ("Yo, Rogaine, yer wiener is ready!"), when I had learned that the peculiar mix of dust from city park baseball diamonds and early December snow had a name ("snirt") and those summer rain squalls that only brought down the temperature for a moment before bringing it up even higher were called "freshets" – though there is nothing refreshing about them – when all the guys I met at gay bars bragged about almost being picked up by Jeffrey Dahmer back in the day (a number of men roughly equivalent to the number of churches in the middle ages that claimed to have a splinter of the One True Cross), when I learned that chocolate pudding counts as a salad in the steak restaurants and that there are in fact two Damen el stops in two entirely different parts of town, the thing I thought was: *home*.

But I had lived in the town of transients for too long. I didn't know how to *be* at home.

Despite what I had pieced together from the details above, I kept challenging my own instinct. What *is* home? I remember in Mary Lee Settle's novel *Celebration*, a Jesuit Priest says that it is a place where you can die. That's nice. My problem was this: my job wasn't permanent. It was a four-year non-renewable teaching appointment, and I saw it as a crowbar that could wrench me out of California and set me free again, to roam the earth, like that devil guy in the Book of Job. I treated Chicago the same way I treated San Francisco, and my entire life: as if each day was my last. Nothing but parties. Serious was a four-letter word. If guys asked me on dates, they could expect no more sex from me.

Despite the fact that I can't, apparently, spell "serious", my employer decided to offer me a permanent position. Have you ever unexpectedly gotten serious about somebody who was supposed to be a summer fling? I felt like I was in a Chekhov story, that one with the Casanova and the lap dog lady. I accepted the position with the same trepidation with which those two acknowledged their very problematic love.

Chicago, by the way, was my love, not any particular Casanova. The human Casanovas and I were still "serious-ing up", if you catch my drift.

And now we come to the part of the story where I want to skip the gory details, because Susan Sontag says (and what Susan Sontag says, goes) if you write about something in nonfiction, you are essentially performing an exorcism, and if you write about it in fiction, you intend to let it inform your writing for the rest of your life. I choose fiction for this skipped part here – and you have to admit, it's pretty clever of me to stick an advertisement for my own novels in the middle of an essay. Unless – cue spooky music – this is actually fiction. I skip a part here, but let me tell you about the consequences of the skipped part so I can get on with my love letter to Chicago.

After non-stop parties and then the skipped part, I found myself stepping out of Lakeshore Rehabilitation Center ("The Unexpected Vacation!"™), a newly-minted proponent of the 12-step program. I have nothing but gratitude to the staff of that, uh, vacationland, to the Friends of Bill, to my fellow vacationers, and, most of all, to a certain gentleman I will call Charley, for that really is his name.

Charley became my sponsor. Charley is selfless, project-oriented, and, in his own words, "Serene? Serene like a hurricane!" Charley laughs at my jokes, tells jokes that make me laugh, and has a heart as big as The Heart of Chicago Hotel. Charley has saved my life, and that's all you really need to know.

Except the part where he has this land yacht, The Crown Vic, a former police cruiser that gets about four miles to the gallon and boasts operating windshield wipers so long as you turn the ignition off when you want the wipers to stop wiping, which can be tough when you're on the Dan Ryan, but can be done. Charley has stuffed the seats with empty McDonald's apple pie cartons and Diet Coke cups. Air conditioning and heating are provided by the Ford Discomfortron System ("Are You Discomfortable Yet?"™), and on any given Sunday, there are a handful of new halfway-heard Books on CD with titles like "Obama-Nation", "Why God Hates Government", and "Franco Got a Bum Rap". Yes, Charley is that rare thing: The Gay Conservative.

I know, I know. But if you knew Charley like I know Charley, you'd think twice about dismissing him, because I'm not being clear. Charley is a libertarian. While he has some very rigid rules for himself and likes to pretend he's a crazed tea party kook, he's got a lot more integrity than most of the hippies I encountered in my San Francisco days, and did I mention he laughs at my jokes?

Who knows how friendships grow, really. Have you ever unexpectedly gotten serious about somebody who was supposed to be a summer fling? I was sure my addiction was a summer fling. I was sure my recovery from addiction was a summer fling. I was sure my relationship to my sponsor was a summer fling. But you know what the real summer fling was? While I was able to keep my job safe from my new and terrible love, and my home and most of my friendships, let's just say this fool and his money were soon parted. I spent all my money on goofballs. I'm that kind of guy. If there were a goofball bar, and we were in it, I'd have a goofball, and then I'd open up my wallet and say, "I love you guys! Goofballs all around!" I'm that kind of goofball addict.

There was a time in my life when I pulled down six figures, and would fly to Paris for a weekend with nothing but my passport and the clothes on my back, and make a necessity of luxury: I needed that pair of Italian loafers, or I'd look like a peasant. At home, even after what I refer to as "The Unpleasantness", you would never know I was financially set back by my goofball problem, because I am *fancy*. But for nearly two years, I was grounded. No more running with the bulls in Spain, no more backpacking across Corsica, and no more touching Jean Paul Gaultier's penis in that little bar in the Marais, which is a story for another time.

But Charley, being project-oriented, had a new project: we were going into business. Through a company called

Orion, Charley was going to be a broker for people who run small stores and restaurants and – get this: bars – who wanted to sell their business, and find a person who wanted to buy the business. His brother was making money hand over fist out in Orange County doing this sort of work, and we were going to get in on the Golden Age of Mom and Pop.

This is how it worked: Charley would have printed up some fancy (not *gay*, mind you: *fancy*) cards that read: "Are you looking to sell your business? We can find a buyer for you. Call Orion Incorporated at 773.555.5555." Cream colored stock. Embossing. No expense wasted, because we were a class act. Class up the ass.

On any given Thursday, Charley would drop off three big boxes of cards and three big boxes of envelopes. On Friday, after a meeting, I stuffed the cards, ran them across a dedicated sponge, and bundled them in groups of 25, tallied them, and put them back into the boxes, ready to go.

And on the following Saturday and usually Sunday morning, no later than 4:30 a.m, come snow, snirt, or freshet, I would get a call: "I'm out front." With a pat on the dog's head and three boxes of cards in my hands, I'd step out the front gate and find Charley madly consolidating apple pie cartons to make room for me. If I dawdled, he'd be studying a map of the greater Chicago area. Not just Chicago: ChicagoLAND. Like, you know, Disneyland. "Welcome to Chicagoland!" It says as you leave O'Hare airport, "You're Nearly Legal Now!". We wouldn't move from that spot until Charley had circled a neighborhood or community – Harvey, Chicago Heights, Rock Island, Belmont, or, cringingly, Aurora – and plotted our course.

"I demand to know where you're taking me," I would say, which is both the title of a really creepy Dan Chaon story and my own care for my fate that morning. Would there be a Starbuck's on the way? Would we stop for an architectural tour? Would it be a nice neighborhood or a bad neighborhood?

None of this really mattered. He would tell me where we were going, but most of the places he named were as meaningless to me as libertarian political candidates. Harwood Heights, Hickory Hills, Worth, Maywood. And at 4:30 in the morning, bad and good neighborhoods really are just about the same.

People, I have seen stores and warehouses and salons and derelict ideas for stores; I've seen bars that are still going strong at five in the morning and cinderblock bunker style bars airing out in the dawn; you can feel the air inside cooler or hotter than the air I walked in with my packets of note cards, carrying the smell of cigarette butts, stale beer, and broken dreams. I have seen walks of shame that will make you feel good about your walk of shame.

We'd often come with a second helper, another recovering goofball addict. I have fondest memories of Tony, may he rest in peace, who liked to do imitations of people in the 12-step meeting from the night before. Tony cut my hair and cleaned my house and showed how my dog, too, with the right kind and amount of food, could inflate rapidly like Kirstie Allie, and got my car towed ("the car got towed", he wrote in an email from the delirium of a relapse, the way Nixon said, "Mistakes were made") and watched "Ultimate Fighting" in the same spirit I watched it. He had been high since he was sixteen and now he was approaching forty and just learning about normal human emotions. I am glad he figured some things out; I am sorry he is gone.

Anyhoo, Tony would take the west side of the street and I would take the east. If it was cold, we'd put on disposable gloves with the fingers cut for good tactile sense. Each and every store, shop, gas station, day care facility, Thai restaurant, and bakery (oh, the bakeries – oh, the smell of donuts at 5 am when it's cold and your fingertips are numb and you don't have money – it's like frickin' *Oliver Twist*) got a card.

There is an official law in Chicagoland that states that you must not put such cards or mail into an official US Post Office mailbox. So we had to slip these cards under doors, fold neatly and let them expand in the space between double doors, toss them through those accordioning gates that get padlocked. My favorite game was to slip my hand through those accordion thingies and toss the card and make it land face up, leaning against the inner door. I called this move, "Yahtzee!" I do this when shaking my HIV pills out of a jar, and get the correct cocktail combination on the table.

We were put out on the street with about four bundles of twenty-five cards, and walked along while Charley patrolled like a barracuda in the police cruiser. If I were Oliver Twist and Tony were the Artful Dodger, Charley had no problem playing Fagin. "You missed one," he'd point to some decrepit sketchy "art gallery". Nobody got back in the car until all the cards were gone.

Once the cards were gone, he would unlock the automatic lock doors and allow Tony and I to warm up, or cool down. We knew he was happy with our work when he did his imitation of that little exorcist lady from *Poltergeist*: "This block is clean," he would say, and pass his hand over the street we'd just worked.

This seems as good a place as any to say that Charley is not just a big-hearted man. Charley is also generous. He'd slip me twenties under the table at restaurants where fellow 12-steppers dined before meetings, so I wouldn't be ashamed. He'd pay me way too well for writing up website text for his various businesses and proofreading his letters (he's a lawyer by day, a bankruptcy lawyer, who often dropped a handful of cards on folding chairs at Debtors Anonymous meetings). My favorite trademark phrase in Charley's threatening collection letters is, "Govern yourselves accordingly." I intend to have this put on my gravestone. For now, it is only my Facebook status.

I tell you all this regarding his free and easy way with money because he is not a rich man – he carries a wad of bills he calls the "Chicago roll", which I'm sure is "nearly legal", and shows his thrift in the oddest corners of life: the above-mentioned windshield wiper system, for example, or the way he snatched rubber bands from me after I had distributed the twenty-five fancy cards in my hand.

He was right to be stingy with the rubber bands. They were as vital as Robinson Crusoe's knife – I remember saying to the rubber band as I felt the envelopes slip from my numb fingers, as I'm sure Crusoe did of his blade, "Please don't break, please don't break." It is amazing how, when you are reduced to the shelter of your own body and very little else, how little you need, and how the strength of a rubber band can be your lifeline. Rubber bands were also used to tally – one rubber band around Charley's wrist equaled 25 cards. At the end, it was fun, and sometimes shocking, to find we had dropped cards in over 500 stores by the time most normal human beings were crawling out of bed.

I came to love what we called "Shitty little strip malls". "Let's go to Maywood," Charley would promise, if I was grumpy about something, like his turning the ignition off on the Dan Ryan, "It's full of shitty little strip malls." I liked them because the stores were close together, and I could drop more cards per hour.

I came to understand the health of a neighborhood by the sturdiness of the doors, the number of empty shops in a shitty little strip mall, the friendliness or ferociousness of the hostess in the local pancake diner. I was fascinated by "hybrid" stores that sold Indian food and pizza, auto tires and porn, waffles and bait. When I dropped a note at any number of day care facilities, we would "fix" the name from "Tiny Tots Play Time" to "Tiny Tots Play Time and Rendering Factory". Charley and I are in love with the nearly legal history of Chicago, a Chicago built by robber barons and child labor and re-routed rivers and rendering factories. Nearly legal, at best. All of this, with the endless quips and color commentary, was my Chicago education. I know, as the song goes, every engineer on every train, all of their children, and all of their names, and every handout in every town, and every lock that ain't locked when no-one's around.

I know where you can find a plaque on a corner that reads, "All Belgians Are Equal". I know where the neo-Nazis hang out in Harwood Heights. I know a beauty salon called

"Sardonyx", where you really have to wonder when some-body in the shop says, "Nice hairdo." I know a lighting store called "Sybarano" that sells lighting fixtures that would make Liberace puke. And basically, I have walked hundreds of miles in Chicago, when you were all asleep. Who knew you could travel so much, when you're grounded?

If I got lost on those long walks, Charley was always near-by, in the Crown Vic, a former police vehicle, which does not so much drive as patrol, like a barracuda. I watched sketchy young men duck behind bushes as we approached, and had to laugh, because we often had to explain ourselves to lily white suburban police cars who wanted to know what we were up to. And Charley, who had lived in a halfway house and became its primary organizer, would sometimes frown in sadness as he recognized somebody from that place, "still out there" as they say in 12-step meetings.

Was this all, then, a search for those still out there? How many walks of shame did I brush past, how many sleazy strip joints were just letting out in the dawn, or tire-and-porn store operations. I have often said that travel on foot is the only real travel, because you meet the road in real time – you have a strong understanding of distances, and difficulties, and bor-ders and geography. And people. And what people call home.

There are many kinds of maps, most depicted from a bird's eye view. Bird's eye view maps are just fine, but I am always haunted by a bird's-eye-view story of Mussolini's son, bombing Ethiopia in WWII, who looked out his cockpit and saw his own exploding bombs as "come fiori" – like beautiful flowers. Distance lends enchantment, and prettifies things that aren't very pretty. You have to get your feet dirty to really know what the land looks like.

There is, however, another kind of map, not so much in favor any more, but of great use to sailors. It's called a "periplum", and if you have ever seen that "*New Yorker* point of view map" where New York City is the center of the uni-verse and everything else in the world rises out of the sea like lumps of stone, you get a pretty good idea of what a periplum is. Sailors used them to find safe harbor when getting close to land. I can think of a no more useful map. Especially when looking for the way home.

Somewhere in my travels with Charley, though the get-rich enterprise didn't really pan out, so much of the venture was a huge success. Serious is no longer a four-letter word. Charley bought a giant house in Iowa , and though I miss our outings, I still text him: "From the train stop in Medina, MN: Angst Auto Services" and he responds immediately, "They only service Fords." We crack me up. I have a friend for life. I, too, have returned to my fancy ways. And I was able to construct a map of Chicago that is my own personal periplum. If I have not found a home in Chicago, I certainly have found a way to it. I can get lost and always know how to make my way on foot. And if the walk is too long, soon, Charley will be sliding up in the Crown Vic, a bundle of cards in his hands, and an apple pie from McDonald's, half eaten.

**FOOTNOTES**

1. "Ohio", said a pedantic would-be employer, "Here, we pronounce that Iowa." No, my dear. "Ohio" is the word Native Americans use for "yawn".

2. Nearly legal.

# CONCERNING THE
# SPECTACULAR AUSTERITIES

## 1. Athletes of God

I N 1996, AT THE DAWN OF UNESCO time when the route had been designated a World Heritage Site but little money had been infused into its "improvement", I walked the Camino de Santiago, sometimes along sheep trails, sometimes along freeways, with a Flemish woman who was carrying all of her belongings in two mesh bags she lifted with rope handles. Her hands were ripped up messes. But she explained that three months before, she had started her pilgrimage with a backpack, which caused terrible back problems. "I returned home and slept in the basement on a thin mat, to keep the spirit of the Camino. My husband shouted down to me every night, don't be a fool and come up here and watch television with me! But I am a penitent. When I felt strong enough, I returned to the place where I stopped and now because of my back I carry all my things in these bags." She arrived in Santiago on the same day I arrived. I felt she deserved her Compostela more than I did. I also felt that she was a little bit crazy.

Seasoned Camino hospitalero Martha Crites told me

about some of her own experiences with ascetics while serving at Refugio Gaucelmo in Rabanal: "One evening, we hosted two different young American men. One passed me a note to get his needs met, but instead of sitting by himself in a meditative way, he sat in the middle of a large group – not speaking – which drew attention to the choice. The third was sweet and funny. He didn't speak until after 8 pm each day! Then he really wanted to talk about past mental health problems which he was trying to walk out on the Camino. So all were dealing with personal problems. I was about to say, it beats doing drugs, but realized that the Camino is a drug." Pilgrim Karen Monteith described a pilgrim who posted a sign on his pack saying that other pilgrims could only sing to him as he walked along, while he only listened and never spoke.

In the preface to her translation of *The Desert Fathers* (*Vitae Patrum*), historian Helen Waddell dismisses "the spectacular austerities which Gibbon (*The Decline and Fall of the Roman Empire*) and his successors have made sufficiently familiar: they are the commonplaces of controversy."[1] But Waddell does not dismiss, of course, before she makes a long list of the bizarre things the ascetics have done in the name of God and spiritual fanaticism: hermits sitting on tall pillars for years, living on nothing but locusts or communion wafers, vowing lifetimes of solitude and silence. The pilgrim, perhaps the most recognizable descendant of the ascetics, walks toward the shrine, but also away from the world. The abbot Marcus said to the hermit abbot Arsenius, 'Wherefore dost thou flee from us?' And Arsenius said, 'God knows that I love you: but I cannot be with God and with men."[2]

And note that the root of asceticism, the word, did not travel far from *asceis,* "the training of the athlete"; the desert fathers were described by their contemporaries as the *athletae Dei*, the athletes of God. Dorotheus the Theban put it more bluntly: "I kill my body, for it kills me."[3]

Today, there are tales of pilgrims to Santiago running the Camino like a marathon, penitents crawling on hands and knees, or backwards, or on unicycle; walkers dressing in the garb of pilgrims from the 12th century and footwear just as basic and problematic. Even the standard pilgrim sees herself at a place in a hierarchy of ability and seriousness – serious pilgrims don't start in León; they start in Roncesvalles. Or better, St. Jean. Or actually, Le Puy or Paris or Vézelay. Serious pilgrims don't ride bicycles. Or even horses. As with nature writing in which the act of swimming with sea turtles somehow puts a nature lover closer to God, the efforts of some pilgrims are made to prove they are holier than, well, thou.

The first thing a pilgrim feels after blisters is special. And yet there is another desire, too, of fitting in, of being invisible. We want to both *act* and *appear*. To repurpose John Berger's observation of women in *Ways of Seeing*, "whilst a pilgrim is walking across a meseta or whilst she is snoring in a refugio, she can scarcely avoid envisaging herself walking or snoring." Interviewed years ago on NPR, Willem Dafoe lamented that he suffered "the actors' disease": "look at me look at me why the hell are you looking at me?" Do pilgrims suffer the actors' disease? If you think so, let me spring another one on you: Dafoe repurposed the actors' disease from the 12-steppers' "disease of addiction".

And here I need to insert a non-pilgrim anecdote: I have a friend, now sober, who tells the story of his last drunken binge: Stopped for driving under the influence, he made himself busy by grabbing the open bottles they had confiscated from his car while they calibrated the breathalyzer and guzzling the various last drops from each. "What are you doing?", the police asked, pulling the bottle from his mouth. "I'm going for the record!" he proudly announced.

In Joseph Conrad's novel *Lord Jim*, Jim's first trip to sea was on a boat with hundreds of Muslims heading to Mecca on the hajj. A storm blows up and the cowardly captain encourages his crew to abandon ship and all its passengers. When morning breaks, the crew, in a lifeboat, are horrified to see the ship unsunk and all the pilgrims standing on deck, a great accusation for dereliction of duty, one that sends Lord Jim on his own aimless pilgrimage to self-worth. Marlowe, who narrates Jim's story, calls the eponymous character "one of us",[4] and as pilgrims, when any of the "us" wander off and don't stick with the ship, we become suspect. Here's a man who lives a life of danger. Everywhere he goes, he stays a stranger. Can we be both things, part of a group and on our own?

Certainly, the reasons for walking differ from pilgrim to pilgrim. Jewish youth is invited to take the birthright "Aliyah" to Israel, but there are several different packages for that pilgrimage – there is a "speed dating" tour so that you might find a significant other to return to, as well as a homeland – after seeing Masada and the Wailing Wall, there's a big beach party in Tel Aviv. Why not? Why can't the methods and intentions differ?

Malcolm X, when making his way to Mecca, wrote in his autobiography, "We were on our plane, in the air, when I learned for the first time that with the crush, there was not supposed to have been space for me, but strings had been pulled, and someone had been put off because they didn't want to disappoint an American Muslim. I felt mingled emotions of regret that I had inconvenienced and discomfited whoever was bumped off the plane for me and, with that, an utter humility and gratefulness that I had been paid such an honor and respect."[5] Like anything truly great and replenishing, we need to approach writing a novel or making pilgrimage or saving the whales with both humility and hubris, an odd combination. But think of what walking actually is. You can see a toddler discover it for the first time – they fall, and then they catch themselves, over and over. All the way to Jerusalem.

Malcolm X's great pleasure was putting on the white ihram, the long white nightshirt and skullcap that makes all pilgrims on the hajj, rich, poor, black, white, equal if not to each other than at least in the eyes of God. The Presbyterians place the bishop's pall over a coffin, so that you do not know whether that coffin is made of alabaster or pine.

We all carry a pack, presumably with the same essentials. Yet pilgrims are always quizzing other pilgrims: how much does your pack weigh? How much did you pay for your shoes? Why are you carrying the collected works of Elias Canetti all the way to Santiago? You will be mocked for carrying a book among your things by the same guy who humped a set of marionettes to entertain his fellow pilgrims every night (another thing pilgrims must suffer). For a moment, the us of us leaves us: your essentials are less essential than mine.

There are already so many things to endure: blisters, cold showers, language barriers, dust, herds of livestock, snoring, weather, walking along freeways, the French. Heather Hemingway writes in the Houston *Chronicle* of students making pilgrimage to Nauvoo, IL, the gravesite shrine of Joseph Smith, founder of the Church of Latter-day Saints, "Giving up their electronic devices for nearly a week, more than 300 youth accompanied by 100 adult leaders, took this pilgrimage for their annual youth conference."[6] Three hundred teenagers without smart phones: now *that* is suffering. To add more seems at once masochistic and uppity. But perhaps that is the nature of the disorder.

Rebekah Scott runs a refugio out on the meseta called "Peaceable Kingdom". She has seen her share of ascetics, real and faux. She offers the best clarification on what's what: "A real ascetic does not usually come to the door unless he's injured or ill, or wants to hear Mass. Real ascetics bunk down in the plantillo, or in the church porch. They mind their own business. When we learn someone is sleeping rough we go and invite them to stay with us, but often as not they are happier outdoors. (When the weather is rough we "compel them to come in." Occasionally the Guardia Civil will deliver them to the door!) When ascetics do stay here, they are polite and clean, often hungry, and they eat whatever is placed before them. They don't ask of things. We have to *tell* them what's available. Not everyone like this is an ascetic. Some are just homeless, introverts, or shy. Once in a while, they're fugitives from the law.

"Sadly, I find a lot of the 'spectacular austerities' on the camino are simply stunts undertaken by people with strange ego needs, with the camino trail as a charming historical backdrop with an accommodating audience. They are kind, holy, and often raising funds for some worthy cause, but fundamentally they are drawing attention to themselves. I know there's a dark corner of Christian history that features this kind of thing: saints who lived atop poles, beat themselves with whips, etc.; perhaps this is the 21st century version, but with a TV crew and book deal thrown in. We had a guy here last year, a media character in his home country, on a 'vow of silence.' Still, his iPad with Auto-Translate was so well-used the letters were worn off the keys. He traveled with a rotating cast of admiring young women. Which kinda makes you wonder. To me, the Camino de Santiago is a holy place. In my opinion, 'stunt pilgrims' are latter-day charlatans, and what they do is an egregious abuse of the camino. When these characters pop up, I let them know how I feel. They are roller-skating down the aisle of my church."

I agree, then stop myself: and who am I to judge? Who knows what struggles are going on inside, mentally and spiritually, as opposed to the struggle of the feet and back? Pilgrim Fran Rossi, who made the journey one year ago, described a fellow pilgrim she encountered: "She was Chinese, born there, but grew up in New York, and ended up in Canada by high school. Super bright, atheist, about 40 and so effing sure of herself about all. We knew her and were social with her, but she never walked with us until the step from Sarria to Portomarin. Yikes, she started getting into it with me, about God and church, but she was so into this punitive thing. She heard that someone carried my pack for part of a day when my feet were bad and she thought they spoiled me, and that God (as she imagined God) would frown upon the person who helped me and even more upon me for being "weak." Well, my other two friends walked ahead while I continued to talk to her. In the end, hours – exhausting hours later – we went down this shorter but funky steep rocky path toward Portomarin. By that time, she had convinced herself that helping was good and that needing was OK. It was the weirdest day."

But we do love drama, don't we? When I signed to write a book about hiking across Corsica years ago, a friend asked, "What do you think you will you write about?"

"I don't know," I answered. "I don't know what will go wrong yet."

Geoff Dyer wrote about Wimbledon as a pilgrimage site in the New York Times Magazine: and because we are in somebody else's home, "We are on our best behavior",[7] he says, though I have heard otherwise from friends who live in that part of London. I think it's important to point out here that good behavior is not necessarily being good. Iris Murdoch points out the difference between the nice and the good. The Conradian "us" of pilgrims always likes to single out the least of its breathren, and if the least drops out of the group, another least will be chosen.

People love to see people *not* on their best behavior. We are, as pilgrims, perpetually the guest in somebody else's home.

I remember the two pilgrims we all loved to hate, the us of us would not allow into the us club, and we called them, jeeringly, Don Quixote and Sancho Panza, mostly because of their build, and partly because they were actually from La Mancha. They didn't mingle much and smelled pretty bad, but that's a pot calling a kettle black. Their spectacular austerity seemed to be refusing to bathe or wash their clothes.

We sneered at their dirtiness and odd social manners – it seemed as if they didn't know how to be normal humans with normal emotions. It was only when we got to the Cruz de Ferro that I finally spent a half a day walking with them, because as they tossed many stones from their packs onto the pile, I learned, through that Andalucian Spanish with its lopped-off endings that they were two recovering heroin addicts who had finally kicked the habit and were celebrating a new life. The stones they threw represented memorials for their several friends who were not able to get clean, and died of the addiction. Learning this fact humbled me in a radical way: I was not the pilgrim that the great Don Quixote and Sancho Panza were.

Pilgrimage is an act that not only balances on a contradiction of hubris and humility, but on innocence and experience, and ideas of home and away. Elizabeth Bishop in her poem, "Questions of Travel", asks the us of us, "Think of the long trip home./ Should we have stayed at home and thought of here?/ Where should we be today?/ Is it right to be watching strangers in a play in this strangest of theatres?"

Pilgrimage is a kind of ascetism, and the ascetics did grapple with a great human problem. Do we get wisdom from experiencing things in the world, recovering it from all the disasters we endure? If so, it doesn't follow that we should seek out experiences that cause disaster – we can't make terror our servant, make ourselves the master of disaster. So much of my experience can be described as bundles of mistakes. Why would I ferret out even more crises to prove that I was unweak? The pilgrim becomes obsessed with being unobsessed. As JV Cunningham, another poet I love put it,

> *Professionals of experience*
> *Who have disasters to withstand them*
> *As if fear never had unmanned them,*
> *Flaunt a presumptuous innocence.*
> *I have preferred indifference.*[8]

What then, might I suggest as an antidote to all these spectacular austerities? In the end, after all, they must be put, in a terrible irony, into the category not of ascetism but of decadence, for only those able to *afford* the extravagances of crazy self-denying diets and revolting abstinence can commit them, and presume themselves innocent. The answer lies in what modern pilgrims have removed from our journey: the long walk home.

## 2. To Seek the Holy Blissful Martyr When They Were Sick

For nearly a thousand years, pilgrims made their slow, wandering way to Santiago de Compostela – my first and most profound long walk – but also had to make their slow, wandering way back home. The elation of arriving at Santiago, at celebrating with fellow pilgrims, and perhaps proceeding to the end of the earth in Finisterre has, for modern pilgrims, been capped with a relatively quick plane ride home. And somehow, perhaps because of that quick ride home, I have felt as if I should still be on the trail – something feels forever unfinished. I'll never forget my months-long readjustment to civilian life after my first walk to that shrine: throwing everything in the basement away, suggesting to friends that we walk to the movies, a mere four miles away, and the pacing, always the pacing, around the perimeters of a room, like a panther in a cage. I hated the way the calluses on my feet and hands melted back to softer skin. I missed worrying about whether the plastic clasps and buckles on my backpack might break. Perhaps the most macho austerity is having the guts to finish the pilgrimage and say it is completed.

Chaucer had big plans for his Canterbury Tales, but I don't think one of those plans was actually finishing the project. There were 29 pilgrims, and each pilgrim was asked to tell 4 tales, two going to Canterbury, and two on the return. A projected 116 stories. That would be a lot of tales. It is fun to imagine what he might have done had he lived past the age of 60. I would especially like to hear the tales told on the return, when the pilgrim mind wasn't turned toward the worldly life lived before visiting the blessed holy martyr and instead, transformed by the experience of a physical and spiritual journey. I have a funny notion that, on the road home, they would have told stories about the fellow pilgrims, no less naughty, but perhaps less hateful. Fewer insults between the Miller and the Cook, A softening of the Knight's holier-than-thous. I think they would tell tales of body-damage brinksmanship, about who had the most blisters and who got sick on too much beer after a day in the sun. But perhaps Chaucer didn't finish his set of tales because, well, he was afraid of ending his own pilgrimage on the page.

What sort of things, as opposed to the things you can't stop, do you wish would never end? Epic romances, that one sandwich that one time, those jeans after you'd broken them in and they weren't yet worn out? Your favorite soap opera? Night swimming, rosaries with the red hats on Wednesday nights, tubing down a river, college idealism, the early discovery of a perfect pop song, that big fat novel that just lay open on the table while you read it no-hands and ate breakfast at the same time, a big fat novel in which you recognize everybody even though the story takes place in Naples in the 50s? That night in the summer when the kids were chasing fireflies and the parents were drinking shandies and telling jokes on the porch at dusk, the grass cool and the frogs just starting up?

Each story in the Canterbury Tales, no matter how naughty (and boy howdy, there are some naughty ones), ends, sometimes shockingly, with an "Amen" – as if the entire yarn were a prayer, a long meditation. Some of the endings are twisted toward absolution, sinners abruptly returning to God after a wild night with the carpenter's wife; some of the endings are not much more than a foxhole prayer; but all of them are offered up to God with a dedication, and all of them are set on paper by a winking, nodding Geoffrey Chaucer, who often absolves himself from his own filth by saying, "I'm just repeating what I heard, folks!"

I absolutely love that idea, of stories, no matter how jaunty, as prayers. Yes, yes, there is nothing more difficult, serious, meditative, and spiritually fulfilling than a pilgrimage. But also, what is spirituality? "Religion is for those who fear hell," goes the old saying, "and spirituality is for those who have already been there." That each of the pilgrims gives their bawdy little tavern story up as an offering to God strikes me as something both liberating and true. My long walks have been things both sacred and profane. I am sorry, Marcus, but you are wrong: it *is* possible to be with God and with men.

Arthur Schopenhauer, a humorless atheist, wrote that the column, in architecture, is the symbol of the will to work. "I am here to hold up the roof," says every column.[9] Many columns are fashioned into caryatids, those brawny beings who carry the weight of the building on their heads or shoulders. Think of all the columns supporting a church. Every column, then, is like a human body, so what does that suggest the capital represents? The profane supports the sacred. All of us, all of our actions, all of our passions, all of our enthusiasms, all of our silliness, all of our less than divine qualities, all of our dreams and myths and demons, all holding up the roof of one serious house. It *is* possible to be too serious, too austere. Did you know that tiny scorpions live in beloved old books, effectively preserving wisdom by eating book lice and dustmites?

The Song of Roland, back in the day when people still had the power to memorize things, was recited by pilgrims, to entertain themselves and others, as they crossed through the battlegrounds of that tale; it's hardly a religious yarn. Everybody had it memorized. And it is worth mentioning here that there are nine surviving manuscripts of the Song of Roland, all of wildly different inclusions and lengths, but the one considered truest to the original – that is, truest to the one people told as they walked through France and Spain – is the one full of spelling errors and wine glass rings, the one sloppily copied by a drunk monk who didn't bother to "improve" the story with his own additions and retractions. It was the pilgrims who knew the story best.[10] Pilgrimage and the tradition of storytelling have always been two entwined things.

All along the road, you meet other pilgrims from all parts of the world, all sorts of intentions. Chaucer's cast of characters has nothing on us. You walk alongside them each day, and before you actually speak with them, you start to have ideas about them, start to imagine stories about them in your head, and yes, you even start to judge them, mostly misjudge them, until you sit down to a big plate of carbs and realize that they are people wonderfully different than what you thought. This is what happens if you are not foolish enough to make a vow that you will not speak to anybody.

You walk for days, and become friends, and you say, "Tell me stories about yourself. I have, literally, *all day*," because you do! And all those marvelous tales come spilling out, the wild times and the bad times and the sweet times, and while you are telling the tales to each other, you are making a new tale. I will introduce pilgrims along the way between my bawdy tales – pilgrims who I recognized as expressions of myself for good and ill. They are still out there, somewhere, making more tales, I hope.

# 3. Jesus was a Rom

To conclude, I offer an anecdote from the beginning of my first pilgrimage to Santiago back in 1996, a moment before the blandeur of the euro, and a moment when I encountered my first and only pilgrim who was actually walking back after reaching Santiago: I had just crossed the Pyrenees with Loek, a man from the Netherlands who had walked from his home. He was seasoned, I was his very opposite. Two days out of St. Jean Pied-de-Port, Loek must have thought I was the dopey naïve American incarnate: I'd come without a sleeping bag (several guidebooks suggested that they were a good idea, but not required), my pack was too heavy, and now this – this! – I'd walked into Spain without a single peseta.

I don't know what I was thinking, except that perhaps Roncesvalles was a town, not just a monastery. I had visions of the way tourist towns go: restaurants that honor Visa, Coca-Cola machines, and a convenient ATM installed in the side of a church. After all, at the monastery in Samos there's a gas station; in one of my beloved photos a shrine of the Virgin rises above an overloaded dumpster. Somehow, to my dismay, Roncesvalles remained more pure.

We'd crossed into Spain on a Saturday. Even if the villages we passed had banks, it was Sunday now, and everything was closed.

At lunchtime in Linzoain, a tiny village that venerated Saint Saturnine, Loek said, "Good thing I am taking care of you," and bought our bocadillos with the pesetas he'd had the foresight to change back in St. Jean. I let him chide me, although I would have liked to point out that he wouldn't have gotten his sandwich exactly the way he wanted it if I hadn't ordered for him. Loek knew a lot of languages, but not a word of Spanish.

From around the corner came a romero, a Rom, with a rucksack. He sat down next to us at the picnic table. I'd dealt a little with the Rom in Seville the year before. If they managed to get their sprig of rosemary into your hands, you were doomed until you gave them money. Of course, I knew all about the practice of mistrusting the Rom, but for El Americano, the Rom were mostly theoretical rather than the nuisance Europeans had made them out to be. I watched Loek shut down, as I fearlessly made conversation with the stranger, practicing my Spanish and asking far too many questions. He was a curiosity, after all. First, he was cross-eyed. Second, he was traveling alone, something I don't think many Rom do. Most importantly, he was a pilgrim, but traveling in the opposite direction, away from Santiago. The perversity thrilled me.

"I'm going to Rome," he explained. "I hope to be there by Christmas." He'd left Santiago on July 25, Saint James's Day. He showed me his compostela, the pilgrim certificate, something I looked forward to having myself. He had a pilgrim's passport, he was for real, but he was going to all the places we had already been to, and he was eager to tell me about all the places I'd be going to.

He pulled out a folded, tattered list of refugios he had stayed in and began to rate them for me. He told me a tantalizing story about the hostel in Ribadixo, hundreds of miles away in Galicia. Next to it he wrote, "Dream of Peregrino".

He said something about rowing out to an island in a river, where the refuge was beneath – what? I was struggling with my Spanish – a trap door? I imagined a wide lake, a castle in the middle, a boatman transporting Christians to safety for a coin. *Arzua, muy mal. Puente la Reina, muchos gentes* (Arzua is very bad. Puente la Reina is crowded). All the way down his ratty sheet, he'd write in si or no. He handed me his list as a gift.

I kept talking to him, and Loek looked askance. He didn't like my encouraging the Rom, and kept studying his own little guidebook. The Rom, whose name was Jesus (I have always found it interesting that certain Latin Catholic countries like Spain and Mexico have a lot of Jesuses, while other Catholic countries like Austria legally forbid christening a child with that name), wanted to know about the refugios in the other direction, what could he expect? Did he have to pay? Would they understand his Spanish? He asked me, "How do I say this in French?" and he wrote on a slip of paper, "Could you please give a pilgrim some money?" In English, sounding as naïve as I could, I asked Loek, "How do you say this in French?" Loek narrowed his eyes and slipped on his backpack. "I am going to get a head start," he said. "Since you are so fast, you will catch up to me soon."

The barkeep came out, perhaps out of concern for me, left alone with the Rom. I wondered whether Jesus could see it, was he used to the world's distrust, did he always get this reaction no matter where he went?

In the Middle Ages, the Rom surged into Spain because of the Camino de Santiago. The pope had given the king of the Rom a letter to carry with them, giving them access to every inn and church along the way. "Please take care of these good people," it said. "They are God's children, and there will be a reward for your hospitality in heaven." The Rom took advantage of this letter for hundreds of years before anyone wised up. The barkeep wanted to know, Is everything all right here? Do I need to get rid of this guy for you? But what he said out loud was, "Anything else to eat?"

I wanted to show I was comfortable with the situation. I had my backpack pinned beneath my knees and if he really wanted my walking stick, I'd find a new one eventually. "*Café con leche, por favor*," I said. I would catch up to Loek fairly quickly.

"*Un bocadillo de queso*," said Jesus, and the barkeep looked at him. But he went in and made the cheese sandwich.

I turned to Jesus. He pointed at the slip of paper again. I said, "I think you say, '*Donnez-moi d'argent*."

"Bueno," *he said*, "Donnez-moi d'argent."

"Si."

He looked at me with those crossed eyes. "*Si. Donnez-moi d'argent*." I laughed, despite the situation I slowly began to understand. "Oh, I see." The barkeep came out with his sandwich and my coffee. "But you see, I don't have any money," I said to Jesus, "Truly, none at all. In fact," I suddenly realized in my absentminded state, "I don't have any money to pay for this coffee." I must have looked panicky.

This is when I experienced my first true Miracle of Santiago: Jesus, my Rom friend, who had already given me his secret list of refugios, pulled a small coin purse out of his pocket and motioned to the barkeep, who stook in the portal of his little shop, draped with that curtain of beads right out of that Hemingway story, used, I guess, to discourage flies. Jesus pulled out the pesetas and motioned at my coffee and his sandwich. "*Todo junto*," he stated, "all together." And he paid for my coffee.

Essentially, a Rom had given me money. The barkeep looked as astonished as I was.

Jesus got up, slipping on his backpack. "*Gracias*," I kept saying, and "*buen viaje*." He said the same to me. I turned, invigorated by unlooked-for generosity and café con leche, and scampered off, eager to catch up with Loek and tell him about the miraculous occurrence. It wasn't until I caught sight of Loek on the road ahead that I realized my pockets were full of francs, a currency now useless to me, but the very thing my Rom friend needed.

**BRIAN BOULDREY**

Of all the pilgrims I have met on the road to Santiago – the Dutchman Loek thrown out of his home by his own wife and told to go to Santiago and get out of her hair, Don Quixote, Sancho Panza, the Flemish woman who carried all of her things in two shopping bags, all of them – the one who haunted me most was the cross-eyed Rom, alone, walking against the flow. His goal had come and gone, and yet he struck me as the more authentic of us, the solitary sojourner who had not turned his back on God nor the "us" of us (in fact, he saw more of Conrad's "us" than any of us!), but had turned desire into longing, removed the object of the end from his sight, and continued, anyway.

## FOOTNOTES

1. Waddell, Helen, *The Desert Fathers*, University of Michigan Press, 1957, p. 13

2. Pelagius, *Historia Monachorum*, Vitae Patrum, volume xxix, *Verba Seniorum*

3. Heraclidis Paradisus, I

4. Conrad, Joseph, *Lord Jim*, Random House, 1899, p. 44

5. Malcolm X with the assistance of Alex Haley, *Autobiography of Malcolm X*, Random House, 1965, ch. 17

6. Hemingway, Heather, "Katy Stake Youth Make Pilgrimage to Nauvoo, Illinois", Houston Chronicle, August 9, 2014.

7. Dyer, Geoff, "The Peculiar Pleasure of the Grand Slam Stands", New York Times Magazine, August 24, 2017.

8. Cunningham, J.V., "A Century of Epigrams #10", *The Collected Poems and Epigrams of J.V. Cunningham*, Swallow Press, Chicago, IL, 1971, p. 110.

9. Schopenhauer, Arthur, *On the Fourfold of the Principle of Sufficient Reason*, George Bell & Sons, London, 1903, p. 83.

10. Harrison, Robert, "Translator's Introduction", *Song of Roland*, Signet Classics, p. 8

# READING IN BED: LITERATURE

"There was a drop scene, wherein sported many a lady lightly clad, and two more ladies lay along the top of the proscenium to steady a large and pallid clock. So rich and so appalling was the effect ... There is something majestic in the bad taste of Italy; it is not the bad taste of a country which knows no better; it has not the nervous vulgarity of England, or the blinded vulgarity of Germany. It observes beauty, and chooses to pass it by. But it attains to beauty's confidence. This tiny theater spraddled and swaggered with the best of them, and these ladies with their clock would have nodded to the young men on the ceiling of the Sistine."

– E.M. Forster, *Where Angels Fear to Tread*

# THE DUCK'S QUACK HAS NO ECHO

ABOUT TWENTY YEARS AGO, I was standing on a stepladder in the home of my ex-boyfriend's new boyfriend's mother. Don't do the math; it's perverse. Her name was Esther, a Jewish widow raised on a Nebraska homestead, a nurse who sewed up members of the Abraham Lincoln Brigade in the Spanish Civil War, and a good old-fashioned Red, who married a McCarthy-ruined member of the American Communist Party. She'd lived from the 1950s at the sidelines of life, watching and reading the signs. We were the best of friends. Each Tuesday after work, I would go to her house, and she would make us a simple supper, and afterward, we would sort her magnificent collection of books so vast they were three-deep in the shelves. Esther sat in her rocking chair with a legal pad and a ball point pen, while I, perched high, read to her the titles and authors of her collection. She had no idea what she had.

An edition of Pushkin's *Eugene Onegin* in the original Russian, inscribed to Queen Victoria. Two novels by Elizabeth Bowen with bookplates stating they were from her own library. Privately printed smut from Oscar Wilde. An entire edition of Darwin translated into Yiddish. Norman Douglas' *South Wind*, printed on blue linen, bound in eelskin. And then this – this! – a novel by Frederick Baron Corvo, *Hadrian the Seventh*, about an Englishman, George Arthur Rose, who becomes Pope.

*Hadrian the Seventh* was part of the Blue Jade Library, a series of books published by Knopf in the 1920s, "designed to cover ... the field of the semi-classic, semi-curious book." These included titles like *The Wooings of Jezebel Pettyfer*, *The Adventures of Hajji Baba of Ispahan*, and *Travels in Tartary*. Esther had one other Blue Jade volume, Ronald Firbank's *The Flower Beneath the Foot*, published in 1923. Esther, my aged, sidelined friend, scribbled down these titles as I read them, and mildly cajoled me to keep up with my task, for she had fed me a decent meal earlier, and I was to earn my keep up there on the ladder, compiling the list of books she'd eventually sell off in order to finance the handicap-accessible room she would need for the last five years of her life, this being the first of those five.

"What in the world is this?" I asked Esther from my perch, finally breaking down, having wasted valuable cataloguing time reading the first page of *The Flower Beneath the Foot* out loud to us both.

I can't help think, now, that this was a setup. She knew I would find this book there on the top shelf, two deep, fifth from the end. Esther knew that she had found another who would watch from the margins, a kindred spirit. "Oh, that weirdo," she said. She told me some details of Firbank's life, a sort of Little Lord Fauntleroy who lived in the nicest suites of Europe's luxury hotels, survived for months on a diet of nothing but peaches and champagne, composed all of his novels on the backs of postcards, impressed his acquaintances (at least two Waughs, a Huxley or so, and a handful of Sitwells) as the most sickly timid pantywaist that Edwardian England could breed; and yet, for all of that, Firbank tirelessly traveled the world and, being neither fish nor fowl, as much in the margins as Esther or myself, manifested in his novels a vision of a world in which everybody was silly – not just him. "You should keep that one," said Esther. "Enjoy!"

That night, I climbed into the bathtub, lit a couple of candles, and became, accidentally, a character in the novel I was reading. "Lying amid the dissolving bath crystals while his manservant deftly bathed him, he fell into a sort of coma, sweet as a religious trance. Beneath the rhythmic sponge, perfumed with *Kiki*, he was St Sebastian, and as the water became cloudier, and the crystals evaporated amid the steam, he was Teresa."

I read until dawn the story (in the case of Firbank, that word, "story", like "theme", "baroque", and "satire" confines his work to an irrelevant regularity) of the courtesan, Mademoiselle de Nazianzi, who loves, in vain, the handsome Prince Yousef ("He has such strength! One could niche an idol in his clear, dinted chin"), the dauphin next in line to reign over some unnamed Balkan nation; she is inexorably led, by every despairingly comic scene, toward the nun's habit. I'm puzzled, wondering why nobody has composed music for a light opera version of *The Flower Beneath the Foot* with choruses of brides and grooms and nuns and priests, full of mistaken identities, disguises, overheard gossip and misheard murmurings, recitative and pitched, congested emotional states, and – my favorite of all – unearned moments of forgiveness, of resolution, of merry naughtiness that somehow build from the ridiculous toward the sublime.

Now, I am not just a homosexual; I am an *American* homosexual. The first novel I wrote was a mandatory coming-of-age story, the bildungsroman being not just part of the gay literary tradition, but the American literary tradition, which I think, in convenient hindsight, is merely or *only* focused on the building of character. The coming-of-age subject gives novelists an excuse for avoiding *shape* in their novels because it looks or seems "honest" – the meandering of a life toward some place, which is usually the end of the novel. Consider Huck Finn, Holden Caufield, and every roadie movie ever made. To stumble upon a novelist like Firbank made me, at first, suspicious, not because he describes characters who speak in nothing but punctuation marks (one courtier gossips, after mishearing His Weariness The King, that "Fleas have been found at the Ritz" and the second courtier

eloquently replies, "...! ...? ...!!"), are born in The Land of
Dates, and have names like the Honorable Lionel Limpness,
or Lady Something, or Madame Wetme (who worships the
god "Chic", "a cruel God"). What stunned me was the man-
nerist approach to plot. I could only compare our shapeless
anti-structured novels to this heavily-structured funhouse
made of cards. Postcards, to be precise.

Detachment is the genius of Firbank's fiction; his characters are all seen at once, and even all their interactions now
and in the future are a solved puzzle, in the end, which I mean
in a gratifying and guileless way rather than a predictable
one. I think seeing Firbank use disastrous dinner parties,
restoration comedy bedroom scenes with trapdoors and funhouse mirrors, creaky attics full of secrets, and cloisters full
of disappointed nuns and priests may seem weird to serious
American readers – myself included – who like our "honest"
autobiographical shapelessness. I think we're so used to
novels being *about* an education rather than being products
*of* them – Firbank strikes me as the opposite of that, trying to
get above all that human scene, to see.

And this, I learned from Firbank, is my own true task as
a gay writer. I have been alarmed of late to hear from some
colleagues that it is necessary for gay writers to put aside
all these rococo chamber novels and write epic tales full of
shameful tragedy and humorless chronologies of unremit-
ting victimhood.

Firbank is not interested in that stuff, and neither am I.
His are comedies – in the truest, Aristotelian sense of that
word. Aristotle's idea is that comedy is "an imitation of men
worse than the average; worse, however, not as regards any
and every sort of fault, but only as regards one particular
kind, the Ridiculous ..." He defines the Ridiculous as "a mistake or deformity not productive of pain or harm to others."
Unlike tragedy, the comic mode proposes that such enslave-
ments are more ridiculous than fatal, and comedy holds out
the hope that a new arrangement of society may provide
some relief. Yes, comic plots tend to be the most artificial,

and arbitrary plot seems to win over consistency of character, but that's because the purpose of a comedy is to improve the culture, rather than improve an individual.

And, that, I think, would be the best thing we gay writers – we gay *gays* – can do to the larger culture: improve it by increasing its scope of manners. In fact, until the 1980s, that is the only thing gay writers *could* do. We showed the world from outside looking in, from our marginal corners, where we could see more. Early gay publishing was not about identity, but individuals swimming in a world that made us feel like monsters. And what fiction is woefully missing, these days, is monsters.

The tragedy of gay writing is that it has been commodified, placed front and center, rather than in the margins, where we have always had a better view. Now we are paid to view ourselves, rather than the world. And if you ask me, the difference between saying "I am interested" and "I am interesting" is the difference between being a hero (albeit a comic hero) and a villain. Firbank's was not a self-absorbed view (at least not on the page), but a view of the world that is so extremely queered that when an ordinary thing, an un-different thing shows up in his novels – a telephone, a newspaper subscription – it shocks us readers, as if we've found a John Deere tractor in the hut of an Amazonian cannibal. "'With us there are no utensils,' murmured the Queen of the Land of Dates." There's a lot of murmuring in Firbank's novels, and therefore a lot that is misheard. "'I couldn't be more surprised,' responded the King, 'if you had told me that fleas had been found at the Ritz.'"

Oh, we would all like to burn with that hard gemlike flame of diamonds, but not everybody gets to be a diamond. Ronald Firbank is not a diamond; he is semi-precious Blue Jade. Blue Jade, as you can figure, is a gem, but not the usual sort – not as valuable, no, and not as common, either, because it's not as often mined. There are more diamond rings among us than there are netsuke carved from blue jade, for there is supply, and there is demand. This is not to say that blue jade is any less beautiful to the eye than a diamond. In fact, I find its hue much more enjoyable than colorless adamant – but I am in the margins, with my own baroque tastes. I have, in the twenty years since I sat at the top of that ladder, reading rarified titles to Esther (gone now, I'm sad to say, for more than fifteen years, but still a love of my life, if of the semi-precious sort), climbed up on other people's ladders and collected up the entire Blue Jade Library, and every now and then I'll draw a bath, ask my manservant to bathe me deftly, and then open up a copy of *The Diabolical Women*, or *Cruel Tales*, or something else by Ronald Firbank, like *Concerning the Eccentricities of Cardinal Pirelli*, or *The Artificial Princess*.

Did you know that a duck's quack can not generate an echo? Scientists don't know why. There are certain writers that remind me of ducks – true, vital, amusing, oddly serene on the surface while chugging away with powerful webbed feet, but their voices will not resonate the way a moose or a wolf might spook us with their reverberant calls as we ride our troika recklessly over the moonlit steppe of life. But ducks can make a difference to an ecosystem. Says Eliot Vereker, a Firbankian antihero in James Thurber's "Something To Say", "Proust has weight – he's a ton of feathers!" As a writer and a reader, in a life of ponderous responsibilities and grim experience, this is the only sort of weight I can bear to lift or foist. It seems immoral to force more tragedy on the world. I endeavor to live by those memorable, if not merely murmured, words of Mademoiselle de Nazianzi: "'O! help me, heaven,' she prayed, 'to be decorative and to do right!'"

Yes, and in that order.

# THE TERRIBLEST POET

## 1.

HIS AUTOBIOGRAPHY BEGINS, "My Dear Readers of this autobiography, which I am the author of, I get leave to inform you that I was born in Edinburgh."

These are the stylings of William Topaz McGonagall, Poet and Tragedian, Knight of the White Elephant, Burmah, self-proclaimed Poet Laureate of Burmah, considered by many to be the author of the worst poem ever written, "The Tay Bridge Disaster." It is filled with forced rhymes and tortured syntax, the stuff that even a child thinks ridiculous:

> Had they been supported on each side with
>     buttresses,
> At least many sensible men confesses,
> For the stronger we our houses do build,
> The less chance we have of being killed.

And you have never seen as many exclamation points in one poem.

Beautiful silvery Tay!
With your landscapes, so lovely and gay!
And the beautiful ship Mars!
With her Juvenile Tars!
Both lovely and gay!
Beautiful, beautiful! Silvery Tay!

The exclamation point has been frowned upon, considered the tool of diarizing teenaged girls and small town tourist information: "Some of the trains were 36 cars long!"

Overused? I say balderdash! I'm with McGonagall on this one!

There are so many exclamation points in life. In fact, they proclaim life! Ahoy! Hark! Westward Ho! Alas! OMG! Ach du lieber! I quit! Happy Birthday! The dog barks! The duck quacks! Rah rah ree! Kick him in the knee! Rah rah rass! Kick him in the other knee! The pilgrims trekking to Santiago de Compostela shout Ultreya! at each other far too often. There is a town in Quebec called St.-Louis-du Ha!Ha! In Melville's *Moby Dick*, there are 1,769 exclamation marks. Almost exactly half of them – 873 – are 1- or 3-word exhortations – "Avast! Consider! The Measure! Fala! Skirra! There she blows! Caramba! Ah God! Right Ahead! All hands! Strong, strong boys! Pull, my boys! Sperm's the play!, and so forth). I dream of an entire novel made of only Stubb's exordium. If you have formal training in typing, you know that you must cross the most distance with the weak pinky in order to make an exclamation mark. It requires intention, planning, and a little extra oomph.

I myself am a trekking pilgrim. I have turned, in my old age, to long hikes – around the Ulster Way, across Corsica, across the spine of the Pyrenees, to Santiago twice (so double the Ultreya!s). This past winter break, I went wandering in the Cairngorms near Inverness, Scotland. When tromping about in northern Scotland in late December, you have to be deliberate, insistent, for the sun sets at 3:45 pm. Despite the brevity of days, the landscape (which must have helped shape the mind of McGonagall) seems that much more crisp, insistent, emphatic: the weather! The mud! The sheep on the hill! The brief sun! The single malt! The snow! The badger! The fox! The pine marten! The song of the crested tit! Yes you heard me I said tit! The yuletide clementine oranges nestled in purple tissue papers in resinous wooden crates!

# 2.

After a few days of hiking through snow and trees, we took a train down to Edinburgh, for I'm an indoor-outdoor sort of guy, like certain Sherwin-Williams paints. The conductor announced we were crossing the Tay, and I looked out the window as we rumbled across the trestles. Immediately I thought of McGonagall.

I have known his Tay Bridge Disaster poem since college, where it was recited each year in the Humanities College "Frivolous Readings" event: faculty brought to students literary texts both major and minor, meant to make everyone laugh, though not always intentionally. E.B. White said that most humor has a shelf life of about 20 years before it goes stale – with a few exceptions. Intentional exceptions like Mark Twain, or accidental exceptions like William McGonagall. So many of my classmates memorized, wallowed, made hallowed his unsophisticated lines, but I believed that if you lied down with doggerel, you'd get up with fleas. I thought there was nothing to be discovered in the unpolished, unfinished, the abandoned, the unschooled, since I was in fact all of these things. I wanted a perfect world without compromise. Learning to love McGonagall has been a journey toward loving myself.

Flying over the water in our modern train, I discovered something a bit grim at the actual site of the disaster. By the pilings of our modern bridge, you can still see the abandoned pilings of the bridge that failed, and cost the world 75 lives, and spawned an absurd poem in which buttresses is rhymed with confesses. Don't say McGonagall didn't try to warn you. As with any chaotic event, it falls to artists to make sense of the stuff, and McGonagall knew his role.

McGonagall is the Charlie Brown Christmas tree of poets. It is fun and easy to laugh at his ill-advised metaphors and unimaginative diction. Apropos of nearly nothing, he also took to the stage, and played Macbeth – but he had to pay the theater for the privilege; when he got to the end of the play, instead of enacting the death called for in the script, he feared the actor playing Macduff was trying to upstage him, so he refused to die.

Yet, dare I say it? I do! – He got a lot of it right in his poetry: tragic and celebratory subjects, the declamatory mode, and emotion, all the emotion an exclamation point can generate. He was never bombastic, he didn't go on for too long (one loves to read his poems even for their terrible choices, and wishes they'd go on just a little longer in awfulness, the way a child wishes you to repeat nonsense poems by Edward Lear or Lewis Carroll), and his books are slim volumes that do not grandstand, like those bards full of their own song, books so thick the title can be printed horizontally on the spine.

And dare I say it? I do! – I am not that much different from McGonagall. He was the son of weavers, mostly uneducated, the first to leave that family trade, just as I was the first in my family to go to college. I loved poetry and chose it as an undergrad major. On the page of the first poem I wrote, my great mentor Alan Shapiro wrote, "Brian, this is a foolish piece of work. You have in this poem the attention span of a hyperkinetic three-year-old." I have spent my entire career and life compensating for my bad grammar, clumsy rhythm, and, most of all, my unbridled enthusiasm. I have never been afraid to make a fool of myself, just like McGonagall.

### 3.

We were leaving Edinburgh in the morning, and the short

day was closing with a cold rain and a sobering tour of The Children's Museum, where you can see a poor child's doll made out of a work boot, three hobnails describing its eyes and nose, and that doll deserves its own exclamation point, if you ask me. Rose, my companion, otherwise curious and adventurous, had had enough of the raw weather. Once again, she said "no" and I was fascinated because it seemed nearly unconsidered. But I told her I would meet her at the hotel, for I needed to make a pilgrimage to the grave of William McGonagall. True pilgrimages, at any rate, are best conducted alone.

Walking briskly in wet boots, I passed many cheerful pubs and monuments to famous Scottish skinflints. There is a bank in Fountainbridge with a gloriously indulgent mosaic, full of decadent golds and blues, spelling out "Thrift is Blessing," the way somebody might spend a lifetime making a lace banner that read, "Reason over Passion." Both of these, I dare say, deserve an exclamation point.

Greyfriars Kirkyard, said to be haunted, has been taking permanent residents since the late 16th century. It is appropriately dark, and there are several graves with iron bars over them to discourage grave robbers. There is a famous terrier said to have stayed at his dead master's grave for fourteen years before finally dying himself. All of this, of course, draws the tourist to guided tours given by people in spooky rubber masks, and attracts Harry Potter fans who wish to see the grave of Tom Riddle, believed to be the original Voldemort. The cemetery is not without its moss-covered tombstone and more than a few grisly skeletons. The ground is uneven from all those caskets settling among roots and rills. It's not a small place, and by the time I arrived, the sun had set and the rain had started to come down.

I thought there would be markers set for the more famous inmates of Greyfriars, but at dusk, in the rain, in an old cemetery, it was more and more difficult to read through the moss, the melting fade of acid-rain on solid stone, and mud, always the mud! I dashed from stone to stone, leaned into the mausoleums. Desperation was running high as night came and hope waned. Where could I find McGonagall? It was a tragedy from one of his poems! Night would make the search impossible, and also creepy.

And then I heard, in the distance, in the dark, near the back wall of the kirkyard, the sound of laughter. It was a tour group under black umbrellas, a chiaroscuro of wicked mirth, and I could just make out that their guide had told them something hilarious. Something hilarious dotted with an exclamation point and much emphatic laughter. The laughter kept coming. It could only mean one thing – they were standing near McGonagall's grave. I had to maneuver through a gauntlet of stones and markers, quick, before the tour group moved away!

Redmond O'Hanlon, in his travel narrative *No Mercy: A Journey into the Heart of the Congo*, describes adopting a baby gorilla orphaned by poachers, and because of the restless crying the gorilla made for its mother, he took the gorilla out for a walk in the thick dangerous jungle. He fell asleep and got lost, and as the sun set on his certain jungle doom, he heard the screams of a village woman being beaten by her husband, a man named Vicky who beat his wife each night, to O'Hanlon's great horror. This time, however, the beating and the screaming were a beacon. O'Hanlon followed the screams back to the safety of the village, gorilla on his shoulder, and all the time, he prayed the terrible prayer: "Vicky ... please. Just this once. Keep at it. Keep beating her." I said a similar sort of prayer as I made my way, in the gloaming, toward the jeering mob. I knew they were laughing at McGonagall. I hated them for laughing at McGonagall. I needed them to laugh at McGonagall.

The little group of tourists had hardly shuffled to the next grave, that of somebody called "The Man of Feeling." I stood where they stood, and used the flash on my phone's camera to illuminate the wall, and the ground. I have a dozen photos saved that seem eerie, as I pointed toward places a stone might sit, or a bundle of flowers. All I got was lichen illuminated. I looked up at the twilit wall on which a plaque proclaimed McGonagall's body "near this spot,"

> I am your Gracious Majesty
> ever faithful to Thee,
> William McGonagall, The Poor Poet,
> That lives in Dundee.

Poor indeed! These were his words, but taken out of context, the double entendre regarding "Poor" – McGonagall's meaning of penniless, and our consideration of him as "the terriblest" – a fish shot in a barrel. I watched the laughing stock of tourists trundle away, and I felt protective of the Poor Poet.

## 4.

There are many bad artists, and artists on their way from the depths to the heights. Great stuff does not just spring forth, like a child of Zeus out of his head. Sure, McGonagall had two flat feet and a tin ear ("Alas! I am very sorry to say/ That ninety lives have been taken away/ On the last Sabbath day of 1879,/Which will be remember'd for a very long time!"), but so did Susan Sontag when writing her brilliant prose, in my opinion. Have you never beat on your horn, stuck in traffic, shouting with any number of exclamation marks, trying desperately to get to the grade school in order to hear your daughter's choir concert and her wobbly adenoidal solo? You weep at the child's enthusiasm, at her ability to be game, to fearlessly try, to take off the cool-kid sunglasses and just sing out. "Desperado! Why don't you come to your senses!" There is nothing like a child singing a song about death to break your heart. So it is with McGonagall – in an age in which we are always looking for the flaw, can't we glean the wheat from the chaff, or must finding the flaw *be* our entertainment? Isn't enthusiasm crucial to the making of art?

The questions are as much for me as they are for you. My

personal pilgrimage to McGonagall's grave was to meditate upon my own strengths and weaknesses. After touching the plaque, searching the dark mossy ground for any evidence of flowers left behind by any one like me, I went down to the used bookstores below Greyfriars and found a couple of volumes of his work. I returned happy to Rose, the Lily of the West, at the hotel, and we had a wee dram and toasted the terriblest poet. It was a moment of quiet joy – no exclamation points this time – yet still insistent and emphatic.

# LEAVES OF GLASS

"OH, THAT WALT WHITMAN," sighed a learned friend, both exasperated and awe-fully, "always on the *make*." It is true that Whitman was constantly on the make, or making. It is hard to keep up with him. This on-the-making sometimes looks like devouring, taking it all in, for his "I" is a democratic "I" that, like an animal on the fifth great day of God, exists in the unending present and presence, always a now. And "then" is not now, which is always "here" – and "there" is not "here". Soon we will go there, then. Soon. But now is now.

Whitman always gave it all, gave it all away, as if every effort was his last effort. From the orchestra pit below his stage, you can hear the brassy "Ta-Daa!" at the end of his poems, a sound that reverberates over and over – right now: Ta-Daa! – and now: Ta-Daa! – and again: Ta-Daa! If I had a nickel for every time Whitman uses the word "now" in *Leaves of Grass*. "Now Finale to the Shore!" Think how his "now"s accumulated over thirty-three years of revising and expanding (he never deleted a "now", never retreated) the several editions of that, his masterpiece. Now is bold, now is brave. "Now Voyager depart!"

His boldness feels like bravery, but what is bravery? Is bravery an actual quality, a willed ability to sally forth into dangerous territory, or is it simply a lack of fear? Are we calling Whitman's decision never to back away from his sometimes frank and sensual subject matter a choice when for him, it was a necessity?

There were other poems and stories and letters Whitman wrote, but *Leaves of Grass* was a whole life's labor. To have such confidence, to be so sure of one's own ability and subject to spend a life devoted to one ever-growing project – even if it might not be a success – this is success in life. In 1886, the glass blower Leopold Blaschka of Dresden, Germany, took it upon himself to create in glass every single of 847 North American grass, flower, and plant specimens for the Harvard Museum of Natural History. *In delicate glass*. The way Audubon painted birds, only in glass, only better. When you visit the shabby museum in Cambridge with its uneven floors and cases full of flyblown taxidermy and patched native costumes, then come across the cases of Blaschka's work, you peer down at the febrile filaments of pistils and stamens and pods and bloom and fronds and you can't help but weep at the care and attention that went into such work. Why do such a thing? "Glass flowers are always in bloom," remarked the botanist who commissioned Blaschka to take on this project. The job took the entire working life of his life, and his son's life, too, to complete.

There are other projects, projects like the leaves of glass and *Leaves of Grass* that inspire in both their public audacity and private intimacy – projects that take a lifetime to dream up, execute, revise, expand. Tom Phillips' ongoing recreation of "A Humument"; Frances Glessner Lee's dollhouse "Nutshell Studies of Unexplained Deaths"; Proust's domestic epic *Remembrance of Things Past*; Blake's "Songs of Innocence and Experience". "World making" sounds a lot like empire building. But in all of these cases, the art remains intimate, and needs the intelligence and imagination of the beholder for the work to work.

And the wonder and epic quality rises not from a mighty "finally" but the resistance to closure. "Art is never finished, only abandoned," said Leonardo da Vinci, another world maker. The painter Bonnard would go into galleries and private homes where hung his own work, and pull a palette from his satchel and add a little paint, touch up, revise. Nothing was ever fully finished. Such an endless act of revision is called "Bonnarding". What is worth finishing is also worth Bonnarding.

Whitman loved to embrace the world, but could see and write the big world growing ever larger over all those accumulated "nows", accumulated "nows" layered in to imitate time passing. So eager to get the thing done, but heartily postponing completion, enthusiastic to see it all, make it all, including life. Ta-Daa! The dialectic, the two odd ideas to hold in your head, improbably, at the same time: to be everything and be nothing, finished and unfinished, at once. They called him The Good Gray Poet; prematurely gray, he looked like a grandfather when still in his thirties, cultivated a grizzled look of seniority, wanting to appear – and perhaps be – old before his time.

> Now finale to the shore!
> Now, land and life, finale, and farewell!
> Now Voyager depart! (much, much for thee is yet
>     in store;)
> Often enough hast thou adventur'd o'er the seas,
> Cautiously cruising, studying the charts,
> Duly again to port, and hawser's tie, returning:
> – But now obey, thy cherish'd secret wish
> Embrace thy friends – leave all in order;
> To port, and hawser's tie, no more returning
> Depart upon they endless cruise, old Sailor!

"Ta-Daa!" This poem, from the section called "Songs Before Parting", was published in the 1867 edition, the second of seven editions of *Leaves of Grass*, when Whitman was the ripe old age of 48. That's how ready to be done he was, and how ready he was to go on. And every song of parting he added to this part of the book did not replace this finale, but layered in his enthusiasm.

All of the living, and therefore death, he saw as prematurely as his gray hair, the deaths and illnesses of his brothers, the specimen days of the Civil War, hard life in the city. How the entire lynchpin of his work can be found in that parenthetical about finishing things finally: "(much, much for thee is yet in store)". He wanted to be free in life and free to be dead, which is not death but a new life. Whitman seems to see this life as that of a child, free to play, floating of a toy boat in a bathtub, model building that prepares us for the great shipbuilding and freeing journey across the cosmic sea. But oh, what a marvelous toy boat he floats in this world! Oh, the freedom a real journey promises!

"Freedom!" shout the collective voices of ants, flung into the weightlessness of outer space with that beloved cartoon character Homer Simpson, whose careless hijinx have broken the glass walls of their farm, "Horrible horrible freedom!" "Anxiety is the dizziness of freedom," said Soren Kierkegaard. We call it free verse, what he uses in *Leaves of Grass*, but think of all the constrictions and constructions of tradition he honors and walks away from. In his poems he tiers his sentences in such an oddly festive way, like the delicious, generous, celebratory layers of a wedding cake. Compare his slathered sentence constructions to those of other long-sentence writers, to the calculated rhetoric of Proust's loopy lengthy sentences full of nooks and crannies where the real truth can hide away, or the filmy mindful abstractions of James, or the Biblical thumpings of Ruskin. There are Bible beats in Whitman, too, but psalmic, always songy psalms.

Blaschka the glass flower maker had but one constraint, and then he was free to do the thing however he liked. The constraint was to do it all. What an order! To imagine doing all of all would make a weak heart quail – one can only create the world one flower at a time, one petal at a time, one vein at a time. Now this, now this, now this.

When we place our fingers into one of those woven bamboo Chinese finger traps, the mistake we make is to give it our all, pull with all our might. Tug harder! It's what makes sense, for it is both fight and flight. Like the finger trap, the wedding ring, the corset, the belt, there are things that bind us even when we are free. These tetherings help us know freedom, of verse and of spirit. Death does this. And love.

What keeps our good gray poet from sailing away then, not yet taking off never to return? It's we that do it, I think. We want him to stay and tell us about joyous departure. It is a pleasure, as readers, to join in the collective "I" of Whitman's poetry in order to be defined broadly. We are and did and saw everything, not just one thing.

But we and Whitman know that there must be defining moments, and the root of "define" is fin, as in final, as in last, as in limit. Now finale to the shore, where our lives shall be defined by the moment we leave it. Whitman, on our behalf, is always in the Now before the actual departure, and the tension is exquisite, like the moment in the bamboo finger trap before we give in to the moment of command, to depart on our endless cruise. Let go, let's go. Oh, that Walt Whitman, always on the make. Making poetry, making love, making away. Ta-Daa.

# PHASE & PHILOSOPHY

W HEN YOU ASK ME, "Have you read Moby Dick?", I will not think of the white whale, or Ahab, or even Quee-queg's coffin. There's somebody else aboard the Pequod; each sailor on board has a journey, a tale, and a life that outlives the fate of the boat. Like the alcoholic old blacksmith, Perth.

He doesn't show up until Chapter 112, and he's only on the reader's mind until the end of Chapter 113, but Perth is the man who made the clasps for Ahab's leg, who made Quee-queg's lightning-attractive harpoon, made the boat-spades, pike-heads and lances. He is the war machine. And Perth makes the ultimate harpoon for Ahab.

He is a blacksmith: he makes fire on board a ship, a ship made of wood. How intimate Perth's relationship must have been with Ahab, to know the exact measurement of his captain's stump. I myself feel exposed when I go bowling, because my rented shoe reveals the rather private fact of my foot size. Like a physician or beautician, Perth knows better than any man aboard where the stump started, where the weakness waxed.

In Perth's youth, he was a well-loved man in his New England community, and had a pretty wife and two children. A garden and a church. All was well until he discovered alco-hol, "the Bottle Conjurer". He stopped working. He stopped making money. His family starved; his family died. And still – the greatest horror of all – Perth continued to live.

"Why tell the rest of the story?" Ishmael says – and Ishmael will go on and on when telling other tales – because even the inexperienced know that those who choose the path of extreme experience – soldiers, addicts, Johnny Rotten – expect to flame out. And when one burns the candle at both ends and finds the wick still smolders, that is horror.

When I talk to people about books any more, they have been deprived by Oprah, God Bless Her Soul. "I don't *relate* to these characters," they tell me. Believe me, I do not care whether you relate to the characters. I love books that make me remember them. And because I do not read books to relate to the characters, here's the thing – what if I told you the character I turned out to relate to most is the destroyed alcoholic mad blacksmith on the 596th page of *Moby Dick*?

There is a lovely oblivion to travel. Ishmael knew it: "Whenever I find myself involuntarily pausing before coffin warehouses, and bringing up the rear of every funeral I meet; and especially whenever my hypos get such an upper hand of me, that it required a strong moral principle to prevent me from … methodically knocking people's hats off – then I account it high time to get to sea as soon as I can."

But see there? Ishmael approaches such terrible moods as moods: as a phase. What happens when your phase – vengeance, in Ahab's case, alcohol in Perth's – hardens into a philosophy? Ishmael has a lovely case of wanderlust. He intends to come back as soon as he's in a better mood. That's not Ahab's plan. Nor Perth's. If wanderlust is the opposite of homesickness, the sickness of homesickness is prison, while the sickness of wanderlust is being lost.

I think one goal of travel is to be reduced to nothing, to lose one's self in an open sea; we half expect to die out there. The fantasy is oblivion; at home we want to be number one; abroad, we want to be invisible, a zero. We try not to look at our maps and be spotted as the tourist we are.

Getting lost, like Ishmael, and staying lost, like Perth, is the difference between a phase and a philosophy – when we start doing the same thing over and over knowing we won't get a different result, we prove to have no interest in returning to life. Poor Perth, I say, when somebody asks me whether I have read *Moby Dick*. And by this I mean, poor *us*, poor *me*. And there travels the Pequod, bound for oblivion: there are so many limbs and minds lost and replaced with metal and fire. Every day, Perth works over his open flame on a wooden ship, a danger to himself and others, and has to remember again and again that he has caused the death of his wife and children. Remember, remember – with memories like that, you certainly can't do otherwise. Doing something over and over, like remembering, and hoping for a different result is the definition of insanity. For many of us who outlived all those we left behind, with whom we should have gone too, memory is madness.

Then what can the hopeless hope for? That some beautiful tale, will transform all the pain. "*Sing sorrow, sorrow: but good win out in the end* …" laments the chorus in Aeschylus' *Agamemnon Oresteia*. And that is what the great novel *Moby Dick* does: turns madness into a painful beauty.

# BED BUGS: POLITICS

"On one occasion (in 1848), Dr. Simpson had an effervescing drink made up of chloric ether and aerated water and served it to his dinner party as 'chloroform champagne'. The guests tasted the drink and found it pleasant but 'heady'. Clarke, the butler ... suggested the cook try some. After drinking a glassful, she collapsed. Clarke panicked and rushed upstairs yelling, 'For God's sake, sir, I've poisoned the cook!' Everyone raced downstairs to find the cook lying on the kitchen floor snoring loudly. Everyone except Clarke and the cook laughed heartily."

— Linda Stratmann,
*Chloroform: The Quest for Oblivion*

# I, ME, WE AND THE GOP

A COUPLE OF TIMES A YEAR, I get together with several friends who all once lived in the same neighborhood in San Francisco. I now live in Chicago, another set left for Boston, and only Jill remains in the Bay Area. We were all sitting around at a recent reunion and Jill was talking about the fact that our old neighborhood, still hers, full of expensive wooden Victorians, has a fire truck that patrols at all times always out of the barn.

"*We* sure do love our fire fighters, don't we?" she asked us.

I told her that since I hadn't lived in San Francisco for fifteen years, I must forfeit the right to use The Municipal We.

I've been thinking about the pronoun "we" a lot lately. I teach a creative writing course in which we look at forms meant to be spoken out loud, but are also considered literature – speeches, sermons, storytelling, prayers, boasts, slam poetry, and lectures. When we discuss declarations and manifestos, we consider the difference between them, that being that declarations declare, declarations call out something that is already there, plain as the nose on your face – both our Declaration of Independence and the Seneca Falls Declaration stand on the sentence, "We hold these truths to be self-evident". There's that we again, the Patriot We, the Nationalist We, the Pep Rally We. *We got spirit, yes we do, we got spirit, how about you?*

In the first typeset proof of the Declaration of Independence created from a manuscript a shy Thomas Jefferson augmented with little quote-like stress marks so that he knew when to stress and when to pause. So, the first proof of the Declaration looks like a sarcastic comedian's script. We hold these truths to be self-evident "that men are created equal".

The "we" in a manifesto differs, for a manifesto makes something manifest that never existed before: the Communist Manifesto, yes, but the statements of all those artists, the futurists and surrealists, the modernists who wanted to "make it new", and all the crazy ones from the Unabomber's caution about industrial society to Charlie Sheen's 11-point manifesto for winning to Lululemon's yoga pant manifesto ("children are the orgasm of life", apparently). Manifestos are more I than We, and a noisy, hilarious We at times, like a misfiring car alarm on a Saturday morning, waking up the irritated neighborhood.

I have mixed feelings about using "we". I have bad memories of being knocked down by grade-school bullies who linked arms and ran me down while chanting "We don't stop for traffic." And I'm a bit terrified of the "We don't like your kind coming around here," which has become a troublingly common We of late. I have lived in Chicago for fifteen years and I don't think I have ever used the Municipal We there, though it feels more like home to me than San Francisco ever did, even more than my home town felt like home. I will chant the Creed We of "We believe in one God, the Father, the Almighty". I am surprised at how choked up I can get when I declare an Alma Mater We, as We will sing thy praise forever.

Northwestern University, my alma mater and employer (there it is), has two fight songs, "Go U Northwestern", which we sing when we get a touchdown, and one called "Push On", which is what we sing when we don't get a first down. "Push on, Northwestern, we'll always stand by you," we promise, the way Nancy promises to stand by Bill Sykes in *Oliver Twist*. I was at a game last Saturday and we were not winning and my old friend Jenny was watching far away on television. We had been in marching band together back in the 1980s when Northwestern broke the record for most consecutive losses. The Loser We will bind people together for life. Jenny and I know "Push On" much better than "Go U Northwestern". Saturday, watching the loss in the bleachers, I got a foreboding text from her, in another state: "Gosh, we sure are playing Push On a lot".

There is the Royal We of queens and popes and threatening lawfirms. And the Nuptial We of married couples is, as Joan Didion described it, the classic betrayal, though the classic betrayal itself can be betrayed. When my mother tells my father, "We Need to Redecorate the Guest Room", she doesn't mean we, she means you, and when my father asks my mother, "Are We Out of Beer?", he doesn't mean we, he means I. Sometimes, there was never a We involved in the first place.

And there is the Memorial We. The Memorial We is a We that connects the present and the absent. I feel the Memorial We most strongly around Arlington or the Vietnam Memorial or the AIDS quilt, where most of the We are far away, but the multitude of names surrounds us, where pronouns become proper nouns, names, thousands of names.

It's not coincidental, I think, that most of the secular and sacred saints we venerate now went charging against the grain of the Municipal We. They are the mad ones who make the manifestos. Janis Joplin was not loved in her native Port Arthur, Texas when she was alive, but they sure like her now, judging from the big statue in the town's front yard. The Little Rock 9 were threatened for daring to integrate Arkansas schools, but now the high school that hated them is a museum in their honor, and a place to which civil rights advocates make pilgrimage every year.

This year, pilgrims marched to the grave of the late Portuguese diplomat Aristide de Sousa Mendes, who saved 30,000 Jews from the Nazis, an estimated 28,800 more than Schindler, much more famous for his list. Because de Sousa Mendes consciously refused to obey the orders of Salazar and the

Fascist We by frantically issuing visas to those 30,000 people, he was found guilty and dismissed from the diplomatic service. He was stripped of his pension and lived in poverty until his death in 1954.

I have, as a Catholic, thought quite a bit about the saints of my religion. I imagine that in those early days of the Church there must have been in every village an especially marvelous person, a person who helped the We of us, maybe led the community, maybe would fix your ox-cart and wouldn't accept payment, gave extra tomatoes from her garden, told a good story. Then that person would die, and they would leave a huge, gaping hole in the fabric of the village, and the people would miss her so keenly that they just knew that person was close to God.

I used to think God was probably too vast for the imagination of the early Christians, but now I know that God is too vast for my imagination, else what's a heaven for? God kept spilling out of the mind's frame, denying his faithful a sense of perfection, of wholeness, by putting it in heaven. What makeshift mosaic one could construct of God's heaven came in the form of the good people we all missed, the Memorial We.

Harvey Milk, perhaps the unofficial saint of gay freedom, predicted his own martyrdom when he made a moving pre-taped speech "to be played in the event of my assassination". The speech is full of the word "us", the objective form for the word "we":

> "I ask this ... If there should be an assassination, I would hope that five, ten, one hundred, a thousand would rise. I would like to see every gay lawyer, every gay architect come out – if a bullet should enter my brain, let that bullet destroy every closet door ... Because it's not about personal gain, not about ego, not about power ... it's about the 'us's' out there. Not only gays, but the Blacks, the Asians, the disabled, the seniors, the us's. Without hope, the us's give up – I know you cannot live on hope alone, but without it, life is not worth living. So you, and you, and you

... You gotta give 'em hope."

This is how an I becomes a we, how a minority becomes a majority.

They are not all dead – some are far more elusive than that. Here's the story of a secular saint, perhaps an accidental saint, who wants to remain anonymous. My friend Lara was recently at a cocktail party of old lefties, attended, in particular, by a lot of old Chicago Weather Underground activists. Many of them are teachers now. You may only remember them as planters of bombs, but they were also very active in helping 1-A dissenters from going to Vietnam. Lara was talking to some of these old activists and thanked them, with a toast, as a group, because her husband was one of those the Weather Underground helped out.

"It was before I met him," she told them, standing in a circle, sipping wine, "before he had his career as a doctor and before he gave me two lovely children. They told him, 'You don't want to go? Okay then. We are going to break into the recruiting office and we are going to steal your file.'" (These were the days before computers, so if your manila folder disappeared, it was gone forever.) "'We will give you a call when the deed is done. When we do, don't contact the recruitment office ever again. Go on with your life.' And then," said Lara, "he got the call, and he never looked back."

A short woman at the edge of the party circle behind Lara said, "Oh, that was me."

Lara turned around and looked at her, "What do you mean, that was you?"

"Well, I wasn't officially in the Weather Underground, but the boy I had a crush on was, and I wanted to impress him. I was the only one small enough to crawl through the transom in the draft office so they pushed me through and I pulled all the Chicago files and destroyed them. That guy was so impressed he finally took me out on a date."

Lara stared at the woman. "Do you have any idea how many lives you've saved? How many lives you've changed? Do you realize how much effect you've had on my life? I never would have met my husband. I never would have had my children."

The woman drained off the rest of her wine and said, "Yeah, probably. I just wanted a boyfriend." And then she slipped out of the circle and into the crowd, never giving Lara her name.

"I kinda want to talk more to her, but really, why should I? Why do we want more from some people who already gave us so much?"

Perhaps we don't want more. Perhaps we just want to give thanks. That is the essence of the Pilgrim We, I suppose.

I dream of a place where the "I" and the "we" are at peace with one another, where the spiritual and the religious, the left and the right, the We and the They, can all hang together in a great inclusive old-school democracy. This might have been the dream of a secular nation that our founding fathers tried to create. I firmly believe in the separation of church and state, but I also believe in the potential good in both of them, separately.

My oldest friend Scott and I were talking the other day about the launch of another one of Elon Musk's SpaceX rockets. "His shareholders must be very happy," grumbled my friend. We both agreed: to many, Elon Musk is a new sort of hero, but for us, not quite a secular saint. Scott reminded me, "When NASA rocketed to the moon, we all went." We still believe, spiritually if not religiously, in the messy experiment of "The Democracy We" after all these years.

# DRAMA QUEEN

THE PROBLEM WITH THE INTERNET is that it is, like your beautiful ex, prescription opiates, and death itself, both the sickness and the cure. Two-thirds of an artist's work is to daydream (which is why, admit it, you hate artists), and most of that daydreaming, in the twenty-first century, involves toggling from the page to various idiotic websites. It is both hilarious and tragic that the apps for blocking internet activity from one's own self, so that actual work can be done, are called "Freedom" and "Self Control". But for a creative person, "fun" and "work" are often the same thing.

\*   \*   \*

Legend has it that in kindergarten, during the "Pageant of the Careers", I was dressed in a policeman's uniform and sang a hymn to that profession, a solo, and throughout the song, I zipped my fly up and down, up and down.

\*   \*   \*

I have no self-control – control must come from outside me. In college, my friends gave me the nickname "Mr. Restraint". They were being ironic. I can spend a lot of time going down various rabbit holes on the internet, and only because of the occasion of this piece did I start to put together the commonalities among the holes. And they are this: I have an almost infantile need for constant narrative in my life. I talk to my friends in little stories. I am delighted when they do the same. I talk to my psychotherapist with anecdotes: "Stop me if I have already told you this one." I am thrilled when she tells me stories about her private life: apparently, she booked a ticket for her and her family to the *wrong* San Jose last month.

\* \* \*

So my favorite internet rabbit holes must be, in some way, little stories. This can be dangerous, of course, the shortness itself: oh, I have time for just one more, I say, until it's 3 in the morning. But I love to see all the short films of babies eating their first lemons, or animals getting onto the field of play at athletic events, or that one video of the guy who says he is grossed out by mayonnaise in large jars but not grossed out by mayonnaise in small jars. But what really holds my attention, in the end, are campy pageants, tumblrs like Crying While Eating, Shitty Wigs in Productions of *Joseph and the Amazing Technicolor Dreamcoat* or Low-Budget Beasts in Productions of *Beauty and the Beast*, and most of all, the bitchy opera commentary sites like Not So Wunderbar, Likely Impossibilities, Iron Tongue of Midnight, or that white zinfandel of gay porn, Barihunks (hundreds and hundreds of photographs of shirtless baritones in operas), and the opera queen's go-to time-waster, Parterre Box.

\* \* \*

To be absolutely accurate, It's La Cieca's Parterre Box, the drag nom de guerre of the editor, writer, and zookeeper of the site, also offering a podcast and a live commentary option for operas that are broadcast through Parterre. The generosity of free content is astonishing, and carefully archived. Its rabbit holes have rabbit holes. She's got broadcast schedules, swag, blog feeds, and, my favorite of all, a complete library of pdfs of issues that appeared between 1993 and 2001 *in print*. Remember print? 1993, when zines were zines.

*   *   *

Opera comes to gay men rather naturally, because of all its artificial qualities. It's not all melodrama, but a lot of it is melodrama. When a gay man is looking at the ceiling, he is not looking at the ceiling. He is *appealing to heaven*. Melodrama is that stepped-up witch's sabbath that feels both lazy and strenuous, a temper tantrum, jet lag. That was what it was like to grow up trying to satisfy an insatiable bully, who stalked me like a villainous landlord: You must pay the rent! I can't pay the rent! Over and over. The bullies kept asking me for a rent I'd never be able to come up with. Melodrama was the norm, the context for everything, disproportionate the way a child's picture of a horse and barn depict the horse as big as the barn, because the child has no experience of normal. AIDS didn't help – when normal meant dying at the age of 30, life made melodrama look like irrelevant regularity. At the height of the epidemic, I knew more than one artist who was employed by a dying but moneyed patron to create some sort of monument to their life: ghost-written memoirs, large-scale portraits, and even, in two different cases, opera libretti. And AIDS made it feel like we were all giving a performance and it would be over soon. Ta-Da! Though I'm still alive, I still experience every project, every class I teach, every friendship, as a performance that will come to an end. Ta-Da! Give me my bouquet, I'll take my curtain calls, and I'll be on my way.

*   *   *

Larry Kramer, that bra-burning Ms. of gay liberation, complained famously that gay men were writing about their lives in too small a fashion, with crummy little short stories and brief memoir columns, while he, of course, was working on a mammoth biography of Abraham Lincoln built around his belief that Lincoln was gay (that was twenty years ago; for all I know, *Gaybraham Lincoln* is still in the works, getting even bigger). At the time he pronounced this, I was the series editor for the short story anthology annual *Best American*

*Gay Fiction*, pulling the majority of the contents from hand-made zines like *Parterre Box*. I took offence. I prefer our stories to be small. Leave the grand for the opera.

\*    \*    \*

Opera is an adult thing, or certainly a thing you need to introduce children to little by little else they will reject them outright, like lemons, or bitchy queens, capitalism, asparagus, Henry James novels, Old Yeller, compromising, naps, etiquette, cemeteries as viable places for picnics, Sylvia Path's "funny" poems, complicated Old Testament Bible stories, and camp (both sorts). Embracing any of these is not detestable so much as it is ridiculous. There is, then, an element of rebellion when embracing it, or a setting apart of one's self, as there is with coming out of the closet. A person must decide that his love for opera is a solitary sport: it's not a lonely place but it is alone. One night in 1992, PBS broadcasted all of Wagner's 5-hour "Parsifal" and my partner, Jeff, sick and about to die, snoozed through it next to me while I made Jordan almond sachets, favors for a friend's upcoming wedding. I was riveted. Jeff would wake up every half hour or so and say, incredulously, "Is this still *on*?"

\*    \*    \*

The fabulously wicked surmise is the only honorable weapon a gay man has. I remember back to the very first issue of *Parterre Box* in which some reader ranted, "Nobody who sings 'Ochye Tchernya' can be exclusively heterosexual." I was hooked. I contend that the precursor to the internet distraction, that first issue of *Parterre*, was a thing called a zine, which you may have heard of. I'm speaking especially of the queercore zines, made from collaged smut, gay radicalization, lonesome niche marketing, pirated images, bitchy mockery, early mortality, and depleted toner cartridges.

\*    \*    \*

My grown nieces and nephew gave me a t-shirt for Christmas that read, "World's Sketchiest Uncle", I felt a curious wash of both pride and shame. I'm the funny uncle who will take you on your first tour of a cemetery, for example, and praise it for its picnicking possibilities, or introduce you to the concept of "human spontaneous combustion", or later, let you try absinthe for the first time. And when I am at last buried in the cold cold ground, my nieces and nephews will be the beneficiaries of not only my absinthe cabinet, but also my library of over 150 books signed by the authors, "For Brian, you were good in bed", and, perhaps most important of all, my extended collection of those queercore zines that were made before they were born, part of the curious scene that started in the late '80s and ended abruptly with the invention of the internet. These include *Dragazine*, *Girl Germs*, *Fuh Cole*, Vaginal Davis' *Fertile LaToya Jackson* (where I first learned about "shrimping", and so will my nieces and nephews), *Shred of Dignity* for gay anarchist skateboarders (admit: that is very clever), and coriest of the core, *Diseased Pariah News* for gay men with AIDS – with an astonishing turnaround in editors-in-chief, *DPN* offered, monthly, a recipe column called "Get Fat! Don't Die!", a special Pariah centerfold, and ongoing instructions on how to be a welfare queen. All of these had a very specific audience in mind, and the budget matched the print run of maybe 200 readers, at times. But the first time I downloaded a page from the World Wide Web, I knew the zine scene was over, and I said, clairvoyant as always, "The internet will make fetishists of us all."

\*    \*    \*

But here's the thing: the one zine that did not die but thrived on the internet was *Parterre Box*, with its roots in the handmade mode back in 1993, and now a clearing house for sassy queer opera fans. A parterre box is, if you must know, one of the box seats on the main floor, In its earliest incarnation, a cut and paste affair with the lurid feel of a ransom note (but all the zines were ransom notes back then), *Parterre Box* declared itself to be "about remembering when opera was queer and dangerous and exciting and making it that way again." And somewhere in its 25 years of existence, it has done just that for me.

\*   \*   \*

Opera has been dangerous the way Times Square used to be dangerous: people from all walks can meet up there. Sure, it's a place to see investment bankers cry. Opera isn't for everyone, but it is for anyone. Perhaps that's why it feels intimate, even when the diva is singing to you and 3,500 others. I recall a dangerous moment in the '90s when Monserrat Caballé was singing La Giaconda and stopped the performance during her big aria because the supertitle translations were making us all giggle. "You should be ashamed of yourself," she accused the audience, and I reddened, hoping she would come up and personally spank me at intermission. Her punishment was more general, and painful, for she did not finish the aria. "I have written a prison scene," wrote John Gay of his *Beggar's Opera*, "which the ladies seem to like."

\*   \*   \*

Go ahead and giggle: opera being dangerous, puh-lease. But when you consider the hundreds of people involved in a production, each one capable of mistakes, you can experience vertigo. One time, Valkyrie Hildegard Behrens fell into a hole in the stage when the electronics misfired in the burning of Valhalla, and though he hated to be the uncruel person writing about it in *Parterre Box*, he admitted, "There are a lot of sopranos I'd like to see fall into a dark hole, but there are just so few that can sing over a large orchestra, and chorus, *for hours*, the way Behrens can."

\*   \*   \*

And the danger is general. I think *Parterre Box* might have survived the zine ex- and implosion so well because opera, too, has a huge foothold in bootleg. The first issues of *Parterre Box* were dangerously peddled outside Lincoln

Center, its founder hassled by security guards; later, the magazine was a conduit for illegal recordings of great performances – various Lisbon *Traviatas*, if you will, as well as contests in which opera queens could do their own performances of mad scenes and mail them in (cassette tapes and VHS format acceptable) in hopes to win … what? The fame of having your own personal melodrama. I submitted once, a version of myself as an unwitting coloratura leading the soprano diva, played by my mother, into her great mad scene. When I talk to my mother on the phone, it is often as if I am just giving her the recitative, with pleasant harpsichord chords backing me up, me zipping my fly up and down, incanting an innocent, "Mo-ther: what are your plans for Thanks-giv-ing?" Chord, chord, then, as the violins and horns swoop, she cries, moving to center stage (never mind this over the phone), tearing at her hair and rending her dress, "Well IIIIII for one, will beeeee a-looone!" and on and on, as the chorus ducks and she goes, Elektra-style, into a doghouse of the mind, and tosses straw and mud all over the stage.

*　　*　　*

Casanova, whose name is synonymous with dangerous pleasure, reveals much about the way people did and did not observe theater and opera in the 18th century. He himself had participated on both sides of the fourth wall, having an early post as a violinist in the San Samuele Theater, and generating crazy sexual escapades that some say inspired the plot of Mozart's *Don Giovanni*. His memoirs describe when Casanova and his friends all went to the opera but nobody ever paid any attention to what was going on onstage. They just talked to their friends, ate, schemed, and had sex in their private boxes. It was like keeping the television on while you threw a party. The theater was a reason for convening – you knew everyone would be there – and even though people could be merciless if the production was bad, they hardly cared if it was good. Imagine trying to sing over all that: that is the life of danger.

*   *   *

Netflix is another rabbit hole, though I hardly ever watch anything new. Just endless re-runs of "Buffy the Vampire Slayer", "Veronica Mars", "Freaks and Geeks" – I always wanted to play the role of teenaged girl. Once, I was with a friend in the Castro with his 16-year-old sister visiting from Baltimore, and one of my favorite divas, the late great artist Jerome, was standing under the movie theater marquee wearing nothing but a loincloth and a birdcage on his head, singing "Nearer My God to Thee" while running his fingernails on a handheld chalkboard. As he got down on one bony knee and opened the birdcage door to apply lipstick, Ta-Da!, I looked at the teenaged sister of my friend and said, "Well, what do you think of our subculture?" and she, between gum snaps, sighed, "Well, you're kinda like me and my friends. Only when you guys watch Beverly Hills 90210, you, like … *care*."

*   *   *

And sometimes we care too much. Besides Trump supporters, opera queens are the only people who can quickly get under my skin. They will sit next to you in the audience and coo or weep loudly, but threaten to behead you if you scratch behind your ear. Every conversation turns into an argument because everybody's an expert at something different: the music, the words, the diva, the production, the conductor, whether Mozart ever wrote melodramatic music ("No, you cretin! There is always the legato line!" – some total stranger assassinating me on some mutual friend's Facebook page). Gay men are very judgmental because everybody, all their lives, have been judging them. "This is the best performance of this aria ever done!" writes one queen on the Parterre Box feed, and just after that, "You are an idiot, this is the worst!" Over and over. "You must pay the rent!" "I can't pay the rent!" Do you want to hear my imitation of two gay men in a relationship arguing with each other? It goes like this: "I'm so sick of your bullshit!" "Well, I'm so sick of *your* bullshit!" "No. I'm so sick of your bullshit," and so forth.

\*　　\*　　\*

When things start looking repetitive, I know it's time to get back to work. But Mr. Einstein, don't get me wrong. Your believe that the definition of insanity is doing the same thing over and over and getting different results, but I believe that's the definition of *rehearsal*. And if you don't rehearse, the opera will suck.

\*　　\*　　\*

When I toggle away from writing this ode to Parterre Box and roam the endless pages of that site, it is one of my many rehearsals. The big surprise, even for me, is that my own personal internet favorites for avoiding work are the favorites that lead me back to the work. For the best thing about opera is that it hits you in your body, and not just in your body, but certain places in your body, strange places. Obviously, looking at shirtless pictures of baritones hits *a* certain bodily place, but don't distract me. The physical response to opera is not unlike the feeling in your stomach when you've heard a good joke and you want to tell it to somebody else as soon as possible. An aria, like a joke, pleasures the body as much as it pleasures the brain. Martin Amis talked about the physicality of making art in his essay, "The Rub of Time": "What sends me up to my study is a feeling in the back of my throat – like the desire for my first cigarette." I don't smoke, but I know, after Tosca sings, "I lived for art," the bodily rumblings that are just as stimulating as the mental ones.

# THE BOY WHO COMES
# TO MY READINGS

THE BOY WHO COMES TO MY bookstore readings is not always a boy. Well, he's not a girl, but what I mean is that sometimes he's a 50-year-old boy. Sometimes he's in a suit and tie, just leaving work. Sometimes he's in his Goth phase and has black fingernails. Sometimes he has brought his lacrosse stick along with him. He sometimes wears a wedding ring. He wears his football jersey or muddy overalls or the bling-bling dazzle of a dozen gold hip-hop chains. Sometimes he really is a boy, maybe 14. His hands are full of other books because, after all, he's here shopping for a few, uh, Elmore Leonard novels. Yeah, that's it. Elmore Leonard.

I will be up at the podium (and don't think I don't see you snoozing back there, or reading a comic book, or rolling your eyes, because at the podium, you see everything), and the boy who comes to my readings will have just happened to be in the store when I just happened to be reading from my supergay book, and he'll have just happened to have been in the, I don't know, children's book section (because that's where bookstore readings always take place), and he'll have just happened to have been looking at *Goodnight Moon* when I read, "And then the boy kissed the other boy and said I love you," or some such thing, and I will see his eyebrows arch in astonishment, making the kind of face that a mother makes if you've accidentally sworn in front of her child.

After this initial shock, he tends to linger. He figures I don't notice him, being so busy up there flapping my gums, fielding questions, thanking the bookstore owner for that lovely introduction. But he's the only thing I see, because I have the eyes of a preacherman for the unbaptized soul who has joined our little storefront church for the first time. I watch him circle the perimeter. The boy who comes to my readings and I see what others cannot: a chalk line on the floor into which he cannot step, because that would mean he was listening; but really, he wants me to think, he's very absorbed in his browsing. He's tuned me out; even when I've said things like "all soapy in the shower" and "that lassitude afterward," he can't be torn away from the flap copy on *Women in Praise of the Sacred*, or that new translation of Thucydides.

After the reading, there are the questions from the audience. How much of this is true? How much of this is made up? I say, "About 60 percent" a second time to the second question, and everybody laughs. The boy who comes to my reading, who can't avoid hearing this exchange, being as close as he is, shakes his head and smiles ruefully, as if to say: Ask a stupid question, get a stupid answer. As if to say: I feel your pain. As if to say: You and I, we're alone outside that chalked-in world of gay lame questions.

There's applause. "Mr. Bouldrey will be happy to sign your books if you'd like to purchase a copy." People start to line up. The boy who comes to my readings doesn't leave, but he doesn't get in line either. At the far end of the room, there's a big stack of the latest book, and a few copies of my older books as well. While the attention of the rest of the bookstore is distracted, and I seem deep in the task of flirting with readers and signing their books, I notice he's looking at the stacks of my book too. Sometimes he makes that don't-swear-in-front-of-my-kid face again when he discovers what he has his hands on. Sometimes he drops the book back on the table as if it has burned him. But he doesn't leave.

The line grows short. In my mind, I have decided: This time, I'm going to talk to the boy who comes to my readings. As soon as I'm done signing books, I'm going to say hello, just a normal, "Hello," and I imagine that it will be all he needs – all the hiding and the nervousness and the wary circling will be over, and he'll collapse. All his not-being-gay muscles will give out, and he will tell me everything, and I'll tell him everything I know, what he might do if he thinks he might have those feelings.

There are only two more people in the line. It's possible he has noticed me noticing him, and that makes him come closer: The chalk line blocking off gay lame questions is gone. Once in a while, the boy who comes to my readings will even get in the line, but not for long – he'll be spooked easily by anybody saying "Hi!" in a chipper upper register.

And just as my duties seem over, that's when the other boy who comes to my readings shows up, the representative from the gay student group at the local university, the budding gay writer with a manuscript, a high school student whose assignment it is to ask a Real Writer what it's like to be a Real Writer. I'm flattered, and we talk. We laugh. I spend too much time. Even the bookstore owner is tapping her toe. Two guys from the front desk are folding up folding chairs with noisy claps and piling them on a dolly. The whole place is shutting down.

The boy who comes to my readings is tenacious, and even through this, he wanders. His skin is burning. His heart is racing. If he reaches out for another book, everybody would see his hand tremble, so he doesn't. He wanders, lonely as a cloud; he doesn't even notice that he's wandered straight into the belles-lettres section, and he doesn't even know what that means. I see his courage beginning to fail, and I make a hasty end to this interview I'm stuck in. Soon I will stand and walk from behind the wall of table and podium, break through the fourth wall of theater, tear down the proscenium arch, and it will just be us, two guys, talking in a bookstore.

That's when the bookstore owner brings big piles of my

book to the table. "Will you sign some stock for us?" I look over at the boy who comes to my readings, and I'm afraid he might faint. But of course I will sign the stock. I'm terribly grateful for their interest in my books, and I would do anything to help them sell copies. The owner opens them up and stacks them, using the dust flap to hold the title page. I scrawl and scrawl and scrawl in a chugging rhythm. She pulls each copy away and slaps a little sticker on the cover: "Signed By the Author". We're a little volunteer brigade, putting out a fire.

By the time the task is finished, everything, everyone is gone: the folding chairs, the podium, the readers, the customers and the boy who comes to my readings. I'm disappointed. But more often than not, a couple of friends are loitering about by the cash register, and they're happy to see me in town, and they want to take me out. We depart, arm in arm, and have a jolly time. I forget about the boy who comes to my readings, until the next reading, when he returns.

The sociology of writing usually bores me; I'm not famous on the gay-writer lecture circuit because I hate to hear myself talk about it. Mostly, the Capital W "Writer" schtick is depressing, for a variety of reasons that endanger the focus of this essay (but I'll enumerate to make my point): I crave privacy and quiet. I want to write, not act. I can't think quickly behind a podium. What I have to say is for the page, not the pulpit. I don't consider myself a pundit, but an enthusiast. When I edited *Wrestling With the Angel: Faith and Religion in the Lives of Gay Men*, I would be asked at readings to offer a bulleted list of ways to reform the Lutheran Church; when I wrote about machismo in "Monster," I was asked to differentiate Guatemalan machismo from Mexican machismo. Should there be abortions? Should Jesse Helms be put to sleep? Where's my boyfriend? How much wood can a woodchuck chuck?

Why would you listen to me? I make a scene: It is not my business as a writer to give answers, but to pose the questions properly. It is not my business, these readings. It is not my business, helping this boy who comes to my readings.

And yet: The boy who comes to my readings has so few opportunities to figure out what it is he wants, and how to go about getting that thing. Especially if he lives in a small town in Kansas, or a tiny university town where people read a lot but aren't gay much. Bookstores sometimes have more gay activity in them than bars or cafés or Internet chat rooms. And wouldn't you rather meet a cute reader than a cute drunk?

Coming out – for me, for the boy who comes to my readings – takes years. It takes years of pushing down desire and watching it pop up in wacked forms. When it finally overcomes the silence, there are the long trails of emotional surprises – shame, enthusiasm, discovery, bad hairdos, suffering, exhilaration, sadness, horror, sarcasm, indulgence, heedlessness, crashing, skirt-gathering, withering glares, acceptance. And after the years of coming out and calming down, there comes the day when one comes out to friends and family. By then, we're in a different emotional state than, say, our parents, who might not have had a clue. I call this the bra-burning emotional state, a period in our lives when we wish there was a Ms. magazine for gays, because then we would subscribe to it.

There stands me, or the boy who comes to my readings, all confidence and nice sweaters, not even remotely a mess, and what is Mom? Mom is a mess. Mom weeps and screams and gnashes teeth and rends garments. And we have no patience for it at all: I'm here, Mom; I'm queer, Mom; get used to it. But see here, my fellow queers – cut this woman some slack. Emotion is not static, like ball lightning. It changes like weather and, like weather, it gets worse before it gets better. Above all, emotion happens in time. You were not always a bra-burning homosexual. You were not always sitting inside the gay lame question chalk circle at the reading.

This has everything to do with writing (you were wondering when I was going to get to a craft issue, since I'm not so crazy about all this sociology). So many gay writers just starting out want to depict themselves in memoirish fiction or fictional memoir (60 percent made up, 60 percent true), which are usually delivered as a monologue or an abstract depicting their first queer kiss, those erotic stirrings for the farmhand helping Pa, or the one-too-many down at the White Swallow. What point of view does the writer take? The bra-burning point of view. What tense? The bra-burning tense. What they want to depict is the way they felt, their emotional state. But what they usually get is the bra-burning emotional state. Nice if you're writing an ACT-UP leaflet; if not, not.

And more often than not, we readers feel nothing. Why? Because emotions happen in time. In life, there is an event, and then there is our response to the event, which turns and turns and turns – the Kübler-Ross anger, denial, fear, depression, acceptance, for example. In writing, there is a scene, with physical bodies and dialogue and smells and tastes and an event, and the characters' responses to the event, and that is the only place where emotions can turn and turn and turn.

Writers fear scenes the way closet cases fear coming out. Writing a scene means making a decision, letting things go. People you invented take on lives of their own. We're so good at making pretty pictures with words. We use summary and description and exposition, dilly-dallying, fence-sitting, toeing the chalk line and pretend we're not at the reading.

And no scene comes out. Or there's a scene all right, a hit-and-run scene in which one character bumps into another one, then goes skittering away, or a scene in which characters sit around and talk and don't say anything, and the writer defends this pale scene in workshop because "that's how daily life is." I'm not saying this is all not so very gay – because when we write all this fluff, what we're doing is what a queen does best: decorating.

We can expose and decorate until our wrists go limp, and we can preach from the podium and we can tell and tell and tell, but every good writer knows that it's better to show than tell, and here's yet another reason why: When you show, you're in scene, and in scene you're in some artistic approximation of time, and in time, readers are able to live with the characters, and feel the flux of feelings. Scenes have movement and intimacy, messy people doing messy things. Decoration is nice, but when was the last time you cried at a painting?

When the boy who comes to my readings finally comes out to his mom, there is a speech, an ultimatum, a now or never (now and never are not in time – and so they might as well be the same thing), and we, as homos, are always furious when Mom doesn't offer instant acceptance.

Well, the other boys who come to my readings, when are they going to get with the program? I must remind myself over and over that we are not all on the same page, nor should we be.

And that's one reason why I never seem to tire of reading, say, coming-of-age stories. I am not made bored or impatient by the endless parade of queers coming out or orphans overcoming obstacles or boys becoming men. Each person is another story, and I can read coming-out stories forever, reinvented with new details, new trails of tears and bad hairdos and other emotional states in various new orders, new dramas and new characters. I love to watch the order emerge from the chaos, the movement of it all, the becoming. I like to recognize that emotion from long ago, refreshed, made to live again with that peculiar mix of nostalgia and invention, which is what memoir often is.

I'm slow to take on the responsibilities of a writer in the world, but I think now that the patience and care I show for fictional characters I create must also be used for the boy who comes to my readings. The truth is, I have no idea how the scene would go if I actually met the boy who comes to my readings. Perhaps he would condemn my big queer soul to eternal damnation. Perhaps he would make a pass at me. Perhaps he would ask me why I never published his great story in *Best American Gay Fiction* and then threaten me with a shiv he fashioned from a spoon. But I can't fully imagine, and I would have no control over the conversation, the scene, him.

**BRIAN BOULDREY**

People, like characters, do terrify me, and so do the things they do, and it's hard for me to deal with their uncontrolled, untransformed messiness. Yes, I'm also afraid of making scenes, but more so up at the podium, doing those readings, fielding those questions, assuming the role of smarty-pants and counselor. But maybe the thing I have to learn is that everybody's the smarty-pants, everybody's the counselor. I can't give up doing those readings, because it is my business. And the boy who comes to my readings, he is my business, too – maybe, most of all.

# FINDING FREEDOM

WHENEVER YOU ASK SOMEBODY what love is, or peace of mind, or a happy marriage, they tend to start discussing these things from a time when they did not have them, or by defining them by what they are not. We have all seen the good thing go bad. The only thing worse than being in hell is being in hell when somebody from heaven opens up the door to hell just to see what's going on down there; and after they see that nothing good is going on in hell, they shut the door quickly, leaving those in hell with just that little glimpse of heaven, that wants nothing to do with those of us in hell. We never want something more than when it has been taken away from us. The opposite of freedom is confinement.

### Confined to

A wheelchair:
> the elderly; Stephen Hawking

Quarters:
> AWOL soldiers, disaffected youth

… these four walls/ Sent inside forever/ Never seeing no one/ Nice again like you/ Mama you/ Mama you:
> Band on the Run, before the run

Bellevue:
> the insane, the addicted, and Carvel's ice cream

cake called "Cookie Puss," apparently, but only on an outpatient basis, so maybe not confined

An island:

dictators in exile, Robinson Crusoe, half the cartoon characters in the *New Yorker*, which makes me think any place insular is some perverse Neverland fantasy of Manhattanites even though Manhattan is an island and Manhattanites are confined to it, they always say, "Why would I leave?"

This Lime Tree Bower, my Prison:

Coleridge

The shadows:

vampires, carnival sideshow acts, Our Forbidden Love

The margins of the text:

footnotes, minorities; strange comments you made in an old edition of Proust about paragraphs like "amazing!" or "oh brother, Marcel" or "6/26/87 3:55 I am getting weepy, getting so close to the end"

Diapers:

the infant, the infirm, the incontinent, certain fetishists

Being robbed of my liberty, deprived of my rest:

that poor sap who dated that damsel fair, The Lily of the West

Being tangled in her hair/ And fettered to her eye:

Richard Lovelace, thinking of Althea, from prison, that guy in the bar whose pickup line for every woman is, "Why did you stop writing poetry?" which works often enough that he continues to use it.

When in your life have you felt less than free? When you ask anybody, they will answer you much more quickly than they would if you were to ask them what freedom means to them. "When I clean," answered Kelly, who usually pays somebody else to do it. "Christmas dinner at my brother Steven's," John laments.

For me, all of high school was a horrible Thunderdome: two men enter, nobody leaves. Miserable marriages, unloving childhood homes, slipped discs, foxholes, bed, old age. Kathy, an old pal from Thunderdome, told me, "I had a horrible marriage and needy children, and sure, I could walk away, but culturally, I couldn't."

There is a there there when we speak of an unfree situation, but there is also time, which is time without time. Oscar Wilde wrote "de Profundis" from a prison term in a dank oubliette that destroyed his health and cost him his life. That prose poem begins,

"... Suffering is one very long moment. We cannot divide it by seasons ... For us there is only one season, the season of sorrow. The very sun and moon seem taken from us ... It is always twilight in one's cell, as it is always twilight in one's heart. And in the sphere of thought, no less than in the sphere of time, motion is no more. The thing that you personally have long ago forgotten, or can easily forget, is happening to me now, and will happen to me again to-morrow."

The work begins with ellipses, for this entrapment seems to have always been happening. The greatest panic about lack of freedom is not having your space taken away, but your time.

A friend of mine, mostly an upstanding citizen just like you and me, who had to go to prison for three months after a drunk driving conviction, said of the experience,

There are no good books. Not even good trash. Weird formulaic Westerns you've never seen in bookstores. And Bibles. They will order you books if you want something, but nobody ever wants something good to read. I put on fifty pounds. And I really felt sorry for the guards. I got to leave after three months. They never get to leave.

Prisoners do time. Guards don't.

I am going to say something controversial now: I think practically everybody in the United States, in the year 2017, with the possible exception of Joe Arpaio, would consider themselves less than free. It's what we all have in common. Whether put upon by other fellow citizens actually or in some bizarre negative fantasy, we are all feeling pretty confined. And not because we are all prisoners – no, it's because we all feel we must be guards. Guarding freedom, guarding our own shameful desires, guarding because there is no damn wall so somebody has to guard the border. Which means Joe Arpaio probably still doesn't feel very free, that ungrateful wretch.

In this, the Land of the Free, we are all feeling very put-upon. We are watched, we are over-armed with guns and fear, we are told how we ought to think (so very much I snarl at phrases like "you're doing it wrong" and "schooled" in head-lines) and what to do. But I figure it's not because we're all prisoners, but because we have set ourselves the unpleasant and endless task of being guards.

My brother is a prison guard. He said, "People don't go to prison for being bad. They go to prison for being stupid." By stupid, I think he meant "high on drugs." Or stupid as in, "anybody who doesn't value the things I value." So a lot of that lack of freedom is rather self-imposed.

Imagine every human in America, and some pets, with their index fingers stuck in both ends of one of those bam-boo finger traps. Tugging for dear life – tugging for freedom. And if you relax, you loser, you will be The Worst American in Americaland. Keep it up! There are certain kinds of confine-ments that will do you no good.

And there are certain kinds of confinements that might do us good. A pregnant woman might choose to be confined to protect a child's life and her own. An addict might give his life over to residential rehab for a time. I was recently con-fined, for my own good, on a psych ward. I went voluntarily, because there were voices in my head. A lot of them.

What were they saying? Oh, you know, the usual: they chanted, "you are a loser because you hear voices" and "we knew you would give up sooner or later." They were right, of course. But they kept me up night after night with their chanting and after several sleepless nights, the voices were even louder.

Let me use Oscar Wilde's "de Profundis" present tense to describe a stay in the psychiatric wing of a hospital, for that experience resides in a hideous timelessness, though it lasted only a handful of days:

It is hard for me to concentrate on what the psychiatrist is saying because I am too busy hating the pajamas that tie in the back, which is what strait jackets do. But the psychiatrist assigned to my case explains my addiction like this:

You are the hobbit. You are in the cave with the sleeping dragon. You're safe now because he sleeps, but you see all that gold, all that treasure. You want it, but if you dare take a piece of the gold, you might set off a little avalanche. That might make the dragon stir, make him roll over. Maybe not awaken him, but are you going to take that chance?

I have had a day's sleep by the time this story is told to me, so it's not going to put me to sleep as *The Hobbit* used to (the movies do a pretty good job making me slumber). His use of storytelling to heal me feels just a little corny, especially when I've made my own way in the world as a storyteller, but today I am grateful for any metaphor. Here in the psych ward, everything is idiotically literal. In the medieval pageant, the parade of figures represent something else – Adam the first man, Eve and her apple of knowledge. In the psych ward, nobody resonates beyond themselves; they are mad in all the different ways one can be mad, and the pageant never ends. Every day, two or three new characters arrive.

When you fill out your preferences for your meal, you have many choices, and you can have all you want, but if you don't circle "spoon" with the stubby golf pencil you have to give back right after completion, you're not going to get a spoon. Do not assume you will get packets of salt and pepper as a matter of course; you must request it. It is difficult to ask for the meat to be cooked rare or to hold the cheese on the ham and cheese. I circle the Italian salad dressing option and receive a packet of dressing – but no salad.

The golf pencils are a brief treat, for the benefit of the kitchen staff rather than us. Even then, they are all blunt. For the rest of the day, if we want to write anything, we have to use crayons. For the first three days, I only write once in my journal, because I am that ill, and I write in crayon, like a child, "THE SHARPEST CRAYON IN THE BOX IS STILL JUST A CRAYON AND NOT MUCH SHARPER THAN THE DULLEST CRAYON IN THE BOX AND IT REMAINS SHARP BECAUSE IT IS THE LEAST USEFUL."

There is nothing sharp on the psych ward, not even a plastic knife for dinner. I haven't shaved because that must be monitored. And while I would like to keep a journal, my hand cramps quickly and what is left of the point of the periwinkle crayon is rubbed flat. I pick up another crayon and work a little longer. I am describing my fellow patients so I can remember not to turn up here again.

At lunch, everybody is friendly, if a little depressed. I'd say four of them are perfectly capable people, but there's something a little too much or too little running through their minds. Every morning, Evan, who loves the San Francisco Giants, meets me as if for the first time, because even though we met days ago, and have discussed our love of baseball and all of his hobbies and family, the drugs they give him just before dinner make him a drooling imbecile, so that each morning, he comes to – Groundhog Day has begun again. Our friendship is a delicate day long, like the life of a mayfly. I am happy to talk to him about the Giants, again. I like to make him happy, which is easy, because I already know before he tells me – he lights up with joy when in the same breath I say Giants and Will "the Thrill" Clark. "I love him too!" What an amazing coincidence that must seem to him. They are trying to come up with the right combination and right dosage of a psychotropic drugs for Evan. Nobody asked me, but it seems to me like they're not even close. In three hours I will say goodbye to him. We will meet again. I envy his glorious blackouts.

What is your idea of hell? Dante's descriptive details

are just that: details. It's his hitting upon the cold idea that there's a God who won't stop punishing, ever, that creates the need for disbelief. I watched a documentary about water babies, in which parents would take their infants into a pool, blow in their faces, and dunk them, then bring them up, blow in their faces again, and dunk them again. This, Dante could only conjure, this endless cycle of trying to catch your breath and never quite recovering. When hiking up hills in high windy altitudes I think of the poor water babies, as I try to steady the gulps of thin air into my lungs and get an unexpected gust from a gale whipping over me. Poor water babies. Poor me. We are in hell.

There's a thin, pretty Pakistani woman hogging the pay phone outside the nurses' station. She's suffering from something called "personality disorder," which is both a vague and vivid explanation for her behavior. She's the stranger who would look over your shoulder at an ATM machine. Somehow she has fashioned a businesswoman's drag by shaping a sari out of her thin blue institutional bedspread and the blue informational folder entitled "Welcome to YOUR Psych Ward" and she has written in golf pencil several phone numbers, and she is ticking them off, lawyers, parents, siblings, old colleagues, trying to talk her way out. If only she would quit struggling, I think. Are the numbers on her folder real? Are the conversations real? What is real in hell?

The Pakistani girl likes to try and take over a lot – your space, the nurse's leadership role, your confidence. She finished uneaten food off everybody's trays when we are or seem done, so I start calling her "The Closer," and saying this to one of the nurses makes her smile against her better judgment. One morning while doing the sit-down exercises, The Closer moves her chair closer and closer to mine until I am forced to either confront her or move. I move. This enrages her. After the exercises, as we head into group therapy, she says, diabolically, "You know that now you've been admitted into the crazy house, you'll never be allowed to own a gun ever again."

I have never owned a gun, and mostly I have never been interested in guns. Suddenly, I have never wanted a gun more in my life. I want any freedom at this moment; the freedom to bear arms will do. The Closer's devil and my devil do a little dance under the new moon.

There's an Asian girl who must have been diagnosed with motormouth, but she's smart and when she talks she talks eloquently and about science and math. She likes to write, too, and we find the least-blunt crayons to share. Only she likes to write on the insides and outsides of Styrofoam cups. She says she likes the feel of the Styrofoam squishing, the satisfaction of the words imprinting deep, as if she is chiseling words on stone. I see her point. She has a lot of hats. She has a lot of clothes. Most of us have been here only a short time and won't stay long, but she has been here for weeks. She would like to go home. Everybody would like to go home.

But there's very little difference between the two of us when we are writing with the blunt stubby crayons. We both look like desperate unkempt detectives jotting down clues, hoping to solve the mystery of what happened.

There is a nice Mexican mother here, a little spindly bird, and she has been self-destructive. I speak a little Spanish, so she talks to me. In the morning during exercise (everybody must remain seated during exercise, lest somebody make a quick run at somebody, so the exercises are the sort that you perform on long plane flights in order to avoid thrombosis – I am pretending that my time on the ward is just a long plane flight), she perks up, like Evan, because she believes today is the day they will let her go home. She is not that depressed any more, she insists. Her husband and children, all at least twice her size, come every day after work, with flowers and candy and kisses, but also with the news that she can't come home, she has to get better. This news, oh my, depresses her. It is a feedback loop and who goes to hospitals to get better? I had friends, loyal good friends, visit me every evening, too. Some patients never get visitors. They watch me chat and laugh with my pals, a glimpse into ordinary life that we privileged people outside that hallway experience, and it is very hard for them to see it. They tell me so.

I am here to sleep. It is what I do. So many borrowed days when I did not sleep, and now I am paying back the days. Just one night, and the hallucinations are gone. Mostly. I can make them come back, even with the dose of Risperidone, but I know what they are and I can, oddly, make them stop. They let me sleep as long as I like, and I get out of a lot of art therapy and spiritual encounters. I feel like I'm taking up a much-needed bed, and my fellow patients sense I'm a short-timer.

LaTonya, a scarecrow of a girl who is mostly fun and a joker and was a ballerina when she was younger, gets weird after her experimental dosage at dinner. She spends the rest of the evening coming on to me. We are watching *Schindler's List* on the big screen television, and one hour in, she pops up and says, "I thought all this was gonna be a comedy." She was going to use the movie's good-time laughs to loosen me up, sitting on the couch sectional piece across from her. Now she will have to depend on her own feminine wiles. She hangs upside down and spreads her straightened legs wide almost into the splits in the air, so that her crotch is unmitigated and the closest part of her body to my face.

She is barking up the wrong asparagus, of course. I would rather be watching the Academy Awards, anyway. You haven't been to an Academy Awards party until you've been to an Academy Awards party on a psych ward. My friends invited me to an Academy Awards party, but I can't even text them to see how that party is going.

I get what I wanted: freedom of a horrid sort. I duck out, disappear, get away. And now I am as confined as I have ever been.

I also achieved what the ancients had quested to do over the millennia. André Breton, in his first "Surrealist Manifesto," defined fanaticism: "The insane are merely victims of their imagination." I had imagined, and dreamed while awake. Unfortunately, when your dreams are layered over daily life, the dissonance is the psychic equivalent of fingers on a chalk-board. Trying to believe in two totally different things – in both dreams and reality, for example – can pull you apart. It is like the disjointed voices of a many-headed gods, we don't know what gesture to heed, which mouth to listen to. That is the overlay of waking and sleeping.

It is my mad friends on the ward who make me realize that I have done something repugnant. I have steered myself to this place, avoided every reality considering it too painful, too wearying, too repetitive, too intense. And here are a dozen people who, taken out of the everyday world that I was through with, are doing everything in their power to get to it. And then one morning at the end of chair exercises, the nurse made the announcement: I would be going home today. I wish he hadn't done that. Perhaps announcing other people's dismissal from the ward is a way of encouraging other patients to work hard, buck up, smile for chrissake. I think it backfires. What could be worse than hell than watching somebody else leave hell?

When one spends enough time controlled or confined, one begins to have the mind of a criminal. I have watched ex-cons walk into the room and have seen them look around to see how everything in it can be weaponized, lead pipes, ropes, trophies, the dumbbells, even Mrs. Peacock's earrings can be something to rip from her ears. When you feel cornered, you feel you need to defend yourself at every moment. And that is exhausting. And that is America: weaponized, controlling, and exhausted.

When I walked out of the ward, I would have liked to have conjured for you a scene from *Shawshank Redemption* – me, breathing in the sweet, sweet air of freedom (which I imagine is the smell of cotton candy and deep fried things at the state fair). But in fact my wings weren't strong enough to lift me into that carnival ride. I took the long way home, on foot, and then on gassy old Chicago buses that labored up hills and gave way for every car and pedestrian. Bus drivers teach me that the way to live in the free world is to always assume that

I go last.

The butterfly is compelled by nature to remain in a chrysalis until its "arms" are strong enough to break out of it on its own – if you "help" it by liberating it too soon, it will certainly die. And so I suggest to you, my beloved country, until and when you are strong enough: relax. We are in some sort of chrysalis as a nation, and we need to let our wings be strong enough to carry us off. And when you are strong enough, let the finger cuff slip off your bound fingers. Confine your control, and control your confinements. In your strength, set yourself and others free.

# ACKNOWLEDGEMENTS

So many people to thank in the making of this book!

*The commissioning muses:* Kathie Bergquist, Jameson Currier, Lev Raphael, Ellen Sussman, Katie Hartsock, Brad Craft, John Bresland, Michael Keller, Tori Telfer, Lyz Lenz, Elizabeth Taylor, Matt Lubbers Moore, Alexander Inglis, Justene Adamec, Christopher Hall, Eula Biss, George Greenia, Raphael Kadushin, Miriam Wolf, Jameson Currier, Ellen Sussman, Brad Craft, Rebecca Brown, Chris Frizzelle, Adrienne Fairhall, Adam Haws, Lesley Hazleton, Jana Navratil, Kathryn Rathke, Tanisha Tekriwal, Rachel Webster, Richard Canning, and Sam Schad.

*The collaborators and enthusiasts:* Jennifer Keller, Tristram Wolff, Dan Chaon, Kelly Luchtman, Will Sonheim, Marta Maretich, Jeff Parker, Stacy Simon, Charlie Evanson, Gwenan Wilbur, Luan Troxel, Kathy Vanderbosch, Lynn Cooper, Scott Lewis, Cate Lewis, and Tara and Becca Bouldrey.

*Jordan Jesse,* his own sentence.

The essays in this volume originally appeared in the following publications: *The Chicago Tribune*: "The Boy Who Comes to My Readings" (formerly, "The Responsibilities of a Gay Writer"), *Blackbird*: "One Singer to Mourn," *LitHub*: "The Shock of the Old," *Medium*: "Drama Queen," *International Journal of Religious Tourism and Pilgrimage:* "Concerning the Spectacular Austerities," *The Rumpus*: "Finding Freedom" and "I, Me, We and the GOP," *Bloom*: "The Terriblest Poet," *Warp & Woof*: "Phase and Philosophy," *Chelsea Street Station*, "Wrestling, Still,", *Windy City Queer*: "Travels with Charley," *Wonderlands*: "Faux Amis,", *Big Trips*: "On Going Back,", *50 LGBT Books Everyone Should Read*: "The Duck's Quack Has No Echo," *Encyclopedia of Dirty Words*: "The Dirty Sanchez", *The Whitman Sampler*, "Leaves of Glass". A bit of "The Good Pornographer" appeared as an essay in *The Bay Guardian*, long gone and well-loved.

**BRIAN BOULDREY**

Brian Bouldrey is the author, most recently, of *Inspired Journeys: Travel Writers in Search of the Muse* (University of Wisconsin Press, 2016). He has written three nonfiction books; *Honorable Bandit: A Walk Across Corsica* (University of Wisconsin Press, September 2007), *Monster: Adventures in American Machismo* (Council Oak Books), and *The Autobiography Box* (Chronicle Books); three novels, *The Genius of Desire*, *Love, the Magician*, and *The Boom Economy* (all three from ReQueered Tales), and he is the editor of several anthologies. He is recipient of Fellowships from Yaddo and Eastern Frontier Society, and the Brush Creek Foundation for the Arts, as well as the Joseph Henry Jackson Award from the San Francisco Foundation, a Lambda Literary Award, and the Western Regional Magazine Award. He is the North American Editor of the "Open Door" literacy series for GemmaMedia. He teaches fiction, creative nonfiction, and literature at Northwestern University.

# About ReQueered Tales

In the heady days of the late 1960s, when young people in many western countries were in the streets protesting for a new, more inclusive world, some of us were in libraries, coffee shops, communes, retreats, bedrooms and dens plotting something even more startling: literature – highbrow and pulp – for an explicitly gay audience. Specifically, we were craving to see our gay lives – in the closet, in the open, in bars, in dire straits and in love – reflected in mystery stories, sci-fi and mainstream fiction. Hercule Poirot, that engaging effete Belgian creation of Agatha Christie might have been gay ... Sherlock Holmes, to all intents and purposes, was one woman shy of gay ... but where were the genuine gay sleuths, where the reader need not read between the lines?

Beginning with Victor J Banis's "Man from C.A.M.P." pulps in the mid-60s – riotous romps spoofing the craze for James Bond spies – readers were suddenly being offered George Baxt's Pharoah Love, a black gay New York City detective, and a real turning point in Joseph Hansen's gay California insurance investigator, Dave Brandstetter, whose world weary Raymond Chandleresque adventures sold strongly and have never been out of print.

Over the next three decades, gay storytelling grew strongly in niche and mainstream publishing ventures. Even with the huge public crisis – as AIDS descended on the gay community beginning in the early 1980s – gay fiction flourished. Stonewall Inn, Alyson Publications, and others nurtured authors and readers ... until mainstream success seemed to come to a halt. While Lambda Literary Foundation had started to recognize work in annual awards about 1990, mainstream publishers began to have cold feet. And then, with the rise of e-books in the new millennium which enabled a new self-publishing industry ... there was both an avalanche of new talent coming to market and burying of print authors who did not cross the divide.

The result?

Perhaps forty years of gay fiction – and notably gay and lesbian mystery, detective and suspense fiction – has been teetering on the brink of obscurity. Orphaned works, orphaned authors, many living and some having passed away – with no one to make the case for their creations to be returned to print (and e-print!). General fiction and non-fiction works embracing gay lives, widely celebrated upon original release, also languished as mainstream publishers shifted their focus.

Until now. That is the mission of ReQueered Tales: to keep in circulation this treasure trove of fantastic fiction. In an era of ebooks, everything of value ought to be accessible. For a new generation of readers, these mystery tales, and works of general fiction, are full of insights into the gay world of the 1960s, '70s, '80s and '90s. For those of us who lived through the period, they are a delightful reminder of our youth and reflect some of our own struggles in growing up gay in those heady times.

We are honored, here at ReQueered Tales, to be custodians shepherding back into circulation some of the best gay and lesbian fiction writing and hope to bring many volumes to the public, in modestly priced, accessible editions, worldwide, over the coming years.

So please join us on this adventure of discovery and rediscovery of the rich talents of writers of recent years as the PIs, cops and amateur sleuths battle forces of evil with fierceness, humor and sometimes a pinch of love.

## The ReQueered Tales Team

*Justene Adamec • Alexander Inglis • Matt Lubbers-Moore*

# *More from* ReQueered Tales

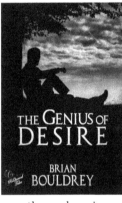

### The Genius of Desire
*Brian Bouldrey*

Hopelessly drawn to the romantic notion of a double life, young Michael Bellman spends summers in Monsalvat, Michigan, coming of age in a loving tangle of highly eccentric relatives: Great Uncle Jimmy speaks to his dead wife during meals; Cousin Anne torments Michael beyond endurance; reckless Cousin Tommy secretly smokes cigars and can't wait to "kick butt in 'Nam" – and Michael watches every magical move he makes.

A few years and one driver's license later, as family alliances change and long-silent desires surface, Michael begins to understand his attraction to the double life because he's living one – at roadside rest stops, in library washrooms, and public parks. Coming out is the first step, coming to terms is the next ...

"A simply told story of a young boy growing into manhood and evolving into himself in the midst of the contradictions, deceptions, denial, ignorance, pretensions, confusions, prejudices, and all the other weaknesses that flesh is heir to ... In one way or another this is the same world we must all find our way through and/or out of." — Hubert Selby, Jr. (*Last Exit to Brooklyn*)

A highly praised debut novel in 1993, this new edition includes a foreword by the author.

## Love, the Magician
*Brian Bouldrey*

In April of 1997, Tristan Broder makes a pilgrimage of sorts from San Francisco to the prickly desert and scalped mountains around Tucson, Arizona, the place where he helped bury his partner Joe five years before. Guided by a comet that crossed the spring sky that year, he wanders toward renewal and resurrection, memory and mystery, deadly secrets and dark intentions.

There are plenty of people in the desert who still love Tristan as much as they did Joe. There's Maria, Joe's wild sister, now a converted Pentecostal; her truck-driving husband Earl; Joe's mother with the dog Murphy she found one day abandoned in the desert; and Joe's best friend Mik, a tough-minded Punjabi Muslim whose one vanity is his long silken hair. With open and glad hearts, they join Tristan to help him make a memorial to the whole-souled man he loved. Yet, despite the fact that they are all bound, like Tristan, by the memory and love for the saint who once lived among them, every one of them is hiding something.

> "Brian Bouldrey's writing is so smart, and so risky, and consistently carries that precarious, curious balance between humor and heartbreak. I'm never certain whether to bust out laughing or burst into tears. *Love, the Magician* is filled with examples of what its narrator calls 'the little node of miracle that every human must have.' It's a really, really terrific novel."
> — Scott Heim (*Mysterious Skin*)

Originally published in 2000, this new edition includes a foreword by Miriam Wolf and an introduction by the author.

## The Boom Economy
*Brian Bouldrey*

For an HIV-positive gay man like Dennis Bacchus, living an active life in early 1990s San Francisco, life was a race against time. New friends were made as quickly as old ones died; it was exhausting, exhilarating and some choices made because, well, why not? Dennis and Jimmy became friends that way until a drug break-through changed everything – an imminent end was no longer certain.

With the reprieve, Dennis travels. In France, a chance train encounter introduces Isabelle, a free-living young woman whose presence shakes up his world. On another journey, with Jimmy and Isabelle, Vancouver and Alaska are included. Inspired to become a Catholic priest, Dennis learns to balance his dual life as a celibate gay man and a Jesuit seminarian, teaching in Minneapolis and ministering to AIDS patients in Santa Clara.

*The Boom Economy* covers what was supposed to be the last decade of Dennis Bacchus' life, but turns out to be the first decade of the rest of it. It's a novel about conversion – all of the social, spiritual, and emotional problems of changing from one life to another.

"I have long admired the wit, compassion and utter poise of Brian Bouldrey's work, his way of finding the hilarity in desperately sad situations, the sharpness and intelligence of his observations of the little details that make up our lives. *The Boom Economy* is the story of a spiritual quest; and a comedy of manners about living with HIV; and an exploration of love and friendship and loneliness at the end of the century. The amazing thing is that it's so funny, so tender, and so wise all at the same time." — Dan Choan

"Bouldrey's diverse and colorful cast of characters, his keen depiction of the complexities of people's psyches, and his deft mixture of the comic and the serious make for a wonderfully rich read." — Philip Gambone

The third of Brian Bouldrey's exquisitely wise, tender and witty novels, it was first published in 2003. Brad Craft provides a foreword to the new edition.

## Winter Eyes
*Lev Raphael*

A coming-of-age novel set in New York and Michigan during the Vietnam War era, *Winter Eyes* shows how the past controls and divides the immigrant Borowski family, and isolates their American-born son Stefan. But when Stefan comes to learn the terrible secrets at the heart of his family, that knowledge transforms them all and points the way to a happy new future for him, despite his doubts about his sexual identity.

A haunting and remarkable novel, *Winter Eyes* is a tale of family secrets, silence, revelation – and the hope for healing and change. A spellbinding achievement from a talented author of American fiction.

"Loneliness, separation, desire and the struggle with gay identity are leitmotifs of Lev Raphael's novel. What distinguishes it is Raphael's handling of grand themes, and his ongoing exploration of worlds both Jewish and gay and how they intersect, daring himself and his readers to contemplate wholeness."
— Jenifer Levin

Lev Raphael is a Lambda Literary Awards winner and multiple nominee for several books. This new 2022 edition contains a foreword by Brian Bouldrey (*The Genius of Desire*).

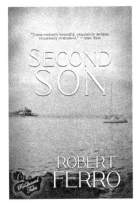

## Second Son
*Robert Ferro*

Mark Valerian, the second son in the Valerian family, is ill, but determined to live life to the fullest – and live forever if he can. When he discovers Bill Mackey, a young theatrical designer who is also suffering from this disease neither wants to name, he also finds the lover of his dreams.

Together they develop an incredible plan to survive that will take them to Europe, to rustic Maine, and finally to the wonderful seaside summer mansion of the Valerian family, where father and son confront the painful ties of kinship ... and the joyous bonds of love.

"*Second Son* is transcendently beautiful; exquisitely written, exquisitely restrained. Its skillfully drawn characters come alive with an incandescent power as they struggle to preserve the romance, the passion, the tenderness that is vital to body and spirit. The accomplishment of *Second Son* reminds us of what literature has always been about – the deep examination of the soul. Rich, poignant, unforgettable, it leaves one with a rare feeling of having been in touch for a little while with the things that really matter." — Anne Rice

"I admired *The Family of Max Desir*. I love *Second Son*. The surprising story of the love between two men threatened by illness is full of fine authentic details and broader realizations about the human condition. Ferro's new work is entirely original, affecting, and yet strangely upbeat and heartening." — Doris Grumbach

Originally published in 1988, it was Ferro's final novel, completed in the months leading to his death from AIDS as he cared for his lover Michael Grumley. This new edition contains a foreword by Tom Cardamone (*Crashing Cathedrals: Edmund White by the Book*).

## Life Drawing
*Michael Grumley*

Born in Iowa to the sounds of Bob and Bing Crosby and the Dorsey brothers, Mickey grows up to the comforting images of his living room TV and the reassuring ruts of his parents' life. During the restless summer of his senior year in high school, drifting away from the girlfriend he could never quite love, Mickey spends a night with another boy, and his world will never be the same.

On a barge floating down the Mississippi, he falls in love with James, a black card player from New Orleans, and in time the two of them settle, bristling with sexual intensity, in the French Quarter – until a brief affair destroys James's trust and sends Mickey to the drugs and sordid life of Los Angeles.

> "A simple, classic, engaging, and beautifully written tale of a boy who ran away from home, a man who didn't make it in the movies, an artist who found himself earlier than most and did it all west of the Mississippi, in places which, while very American, few Americans have ever been." — Andrew Holleran

> "*Life Drawing* affirms the rich complexity of passion in the story of a small-town boy's difficult journey to manhood. Michael Grumley's crisp, direct language brings to life the demanding wonder of sexuality and the delicate tightrope of love between black men and white men." — Melvin Dixon

Originally published in 1991, it was Grumley's only novel, completed in the month's leading to his death from AIDS as he was cared for his lover Robert Ferro. This new edition contains the original foreword by Edmund White (*A Saint from Texas*) and afterword by George Stambolian (*Gay Men's Anthologies Men on Men*), close friends of the couple.

FIDELITIES
A BOOK OF STORIES

RICHARD HALL

### Fidelities: A Book of Stories
*Richard Hall*

The *Los Angeles Times* says "Richard Hall's prose displays a rare polish, and his accounts of ordinary and exceptional lives unfold in graceful cadences." Fidelities is a stunning collection of stories that explores the varieties of gay experience – love stories, both passionate and compassionate; tales of suspense; narratives on the theme of AIDS; even a ghost story. Among the most adept and technically accomplished writers of his generation, Hall's third and last collection of short stories is an eloquent work of immense power.

The author of the novels *The Butterscotch Prince* and *Family Fictions*, Hall's short stories give a sense of having been distilled and polished over time till they glow with depth and wisdom. "Diamonds Are Forever" highlights a gay man and his married sister who are incapable of seeing the shared traits that make it so difficult for them to accept each other; the story's carefully paced wrangling over an heirloom is masterful. "Avery Milbanke Day" features a 70-year-old writer – his seven novels about "the literature of hesitation" long neglected – decides to stay with his old dying lover and nurse him through a final crisis instead of attending a public celebration of his novels and himself. In "Country People" the author presents a gentle, eerie metaphor for the search for a sense of history, reflecting on previous generations of gay men and lesbians.

> "Hall's stories evoke comparison with Henry James or Maupassant, Hemingway and Fitzgerald ... A luminous collection ... Hall has found in gay life stories to amuse, entertain, and move." — *Lambda Book Report*

> "[A] rich, poignant collection ... The ruminations in Fidelities are remarkably palpable, utterly believable. Enlivened by precise flourishes of description, they touch directly on the reader's empathy button, and hold." — *San Francisco Chronicle*

Hall's final publication before his own death at age 66 from AIDS-related causes, this 30th year anniversary edition celebrates his art at its peak. This new edition includes a foreword by Alexander Inglis.

## A Perfect Scar and Other Stories
*Trebor Healey*

This whimsical, sly, and slightly crazy collection of short stories from award-winning novelist, poet, and songwriter Trebor Healey covers much ground. The range is jaw-dropping: from a Vietnamese gangster with a voracious libido and a small boy troubled by his gay dog to an 1870s hermaphrodite cowboy named Captain Jinx … and then there's the lad who becomes a sex-inspiring satyr, an American Spanish student in Guanajuato seduced by a pair of twins during the Cervantino celebrations, and a housesitting gig that goes terribly awry.

There is humor and insight delivered in lyrical, vibratory phrases, and darker more haunting tales as well, often with a thread of Catholic, as well as Mexican culture, involving young men facing untimely death, reflections on aging, family, duty, sacrifice and sibling rivalry – and the fateful and courageous choices we are forced to make in the name of love.

> "Trebor Healey is all soul … The way he stacks sentences vibrates on the page. There's an impressive, experimental range in this short story collection. Trebor Healey uses multiple narrators to bring voice to a variety of human experiences."
> — Kirk Read, *How I Learned to Snap*

> "Trebor Healey's writing is suffused with the purest emotion, the bravest, funniest tone, and the perfect balance of poetics, daring and charm." — Joy Nicholson, *The Tribes of Palos Verdes*

Originally published in 2007, this new edition includes a foreword by Peter Dubé (*The Headless Man*).

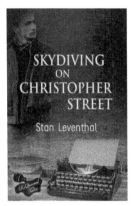

## Skydiving on Christopher Street
*Stan Leventhal*

Like bookends, *Skydiving* returns to the characters and bustle of New York a few years after *Mountain Climbing in Sheridan Square.*

Stan Leventhal paints a picture of Christopher Street in the 80s and 90s. "The streets became ours again. When the fag-bashers began to get bold, to slither from their slimy lairs, the young gay guys and fledgling lesbians fought back. There was a new war to win, along with battles of fear, ignorance, and indifference ... We paid for it with our muscles, our brains, our bodily fluids. It has our names written all over it. Our blood fills the cracks in the pavement. It's ours and we're never going to give it up."

Against that backdrop, we see the pieces of an ordinary life. He's an editor for a porn publishing house – it's not glamorous, it's just work. His relationship is on the verge of ending. He is visited by the ghosts of friends he has lost to AIDS. In the midst of the familiar days, he learns from his doctor that he too has AIDS.

> "A tender, honest novel about that moment between diagnosis and the decision to grow. Messy boyfriends and dreamy crushes set against the back-drop of daily life make Levethal's characters vulnerable and familiar."
> — Sarah Schulman (*Let the Record Show*)

> "*Skydiving on Christopher Street*, is a startling attempt to capture the life of an urban gay man on the printed page. Read in conjunction with *Mountain Climbing in Sheridan Square*, the book moves us into a darker, more disturbing arena in which knowledge does not necessarily bring happiness, understanding does not bring relief. Leventhal's vision is clear and undaunted and, for all of its somber chiaroscuro, challenges us to see the world through new eyes and to revel in its author's ability to translate life into art, pain into understanding."
> — Michael Bronski (*A Queer History of the United States*)

From 1995, this is Leventhal's final novel. This edition features a foreword by Paras Borgohain who is writing a screenplay for the novel.

## Boys Like Us
*Peter McGehee*

**Boys Like Us Trilogy, Book 1** – Peter McGehee's debut novel is a rompish, bed-hopping affair – a modern comedy of manners – in which our twentysomething protagonist, Zero MacNoo performs all the rituals – sexual, familial, and grievous – required of urban gay males in the early 1990s. It is a remarkable comedy about life, love, and friendship in the age of AIDS.

Zero, an Arkansas expat who has swapped out Little Rock for the cool contenporary tones of Toronto gay life, is perplexed by the curveballs of fate. His best friend has been diagnosed with AIDS; Zero is frantic to organize a circle of support. And when Arkansas also calls, it's to support his mother's second marriage and confrontations with the zany array of crazed Southerners he calls family ensue.

"... a gem of a novel. *Boys Like Us* is funny, sexy, tender, and touching – often in the same sentence." — Larry Duplechan

"*Boys Like Us* is an affable, enjoyable story ... McGehee has the ability, through an ingratiating style and witty observations, to transform Zero's everyday life into something we care about." — Michael Bronski

Funny, bittersweet, outrageous, and moving, Zero's adventures make up the first part of *Boys Like Us* trilogy. This new edition is accompanied by introductions from Dr Raymond-Jean Frontain and long-time collaborator Fiji Robinson.

## Like People in History
*Felice Picano*

Solid, cautious Roger Sansarc and flamboyant, mercurial Alistair Dodge are second cousins who become lifelong friends when they first meet as nine-year-old boys in 1954. Their lives constantly intersect at crucial moments in their personal histories as each discovers his own unique – and uniquely gay – identity. Their complex, tumultuous, and madcap relationship endures against 40 years of history and their involvement with the handsome model, poet, and decorated Vietnam vet Matt Loguidice, whom they both love. Picano chronicles and celebrates gay life and subculture over the last half of the twentieth century: from the legendary 1969 gathering at Woodstock to the legendary parties at Fire Island Pines in the 1970s, from Malibu Beach in its palmiest surfer days to San Francisco during its gayest era, from the cities and jungles of South Vietnam during the war to Manhattan's Greenwich Village and Upper East Side during the 1990s AIDS war.

"It's the heroic and funny saga of the last three decades by someone who saw everything and forgot nothing." — Edmund White

"Harrowing and sad, and very funny, *Like People in History* manages to bridge the unnerving chasm between the queer present and the gay past." — Andrew Holleran

In a book that could have been written only by one who lived it and survived to tell, Picano weaves a powerful saga of four decades in the lives of two men and their lovers, relatives, friends, and enemies. Tragic, comic, sexy, and romantic, filled with varied and colorful characters, *Like People in History* is both extraordinarily moving and supremely entertaining.

Published to acclaim in 1995, winner of the Ferro-Grumley Award for Best Novel, this 25th Anniversary edition for 2020 features a new foreword by Richard Burnett and an afterword by the author.

## Something Inside
## Conversations with Gay Fiction Writers
*Philip Gambone*

In the late-20th century, gay literature had earned a place at the British and American literary tables, spawning its own constellation of important writers and winning a dedicated audience. This collection of probing interviews represents an attempt to offer a group portrait of the most important gay fiction writers.

The extraordinary power of the interviews, originally set down from 1987 to 1997, brings to life the passionate intellect of several voices now stilled among them Joseph Hansen, Allen Barnett, John Preston and Paul Monette. Others such as Scott Heim, Brad Gooch, Lev Raphael, Alan Hollinghurst and Michael Lowanthal were just tasting fame, even notoriety and have gone on to richly deserved acclaim. Published near the height of mainstream accolades for gay fiction as a category, Edmund White, David Plante, Andrew Holleran, Michael Cunningham and Christopher Bram had already enjoyed wide readership and two decades of scrutiny and broad readership.

Many of the pieces are accompanied by portraits from Robert Giard who set out, with urgency during the mid-1980s AIDS crisis, to capture gay artists in their prime; these images make a unique and profound contribution to this collection.

> "A rich collective portrait of some of the most important and interesting gay writers of the last three decades."
> — *Montreal Mirror*

Philip Gambone, a wise and insightful questioner, draws out incredible detail, emotion and personality in a context which still makes for compelling reading thirty years on. The author includes a 2022 update welcoming new readers to this indispensable resource.

◌

**If you enjoyed this book,
please help spread the word
by posting a short,
constructive review at
your favorite social media site
or book retailer.**

**We thank you, greatly,
for your support.**

**And don't be shy! Contact us!**

*For more information about current and future releases,
please contact us:*

E-mail:  *requeeredtales@gmail.com*
Facebook (Like us!):  www.facebook.com/ReQueeredTales
Twitter:  @ReQueered
Instagram: www.instagram.com/requeered
Web:  www.ReQueeredTales.com
Blog:  www.ReQueeredTales.com/blog
Mailing list (Subscribe for latest news):  https://bit.ly/RQTJoin

Printed in the USA
CPSIA information can be obtained
at www.ICGtesting.com
LVHW040533201023
761597LV00011B/876

9 781959 902058